Lloyd D Simpson

Notes on Thomas Jefferson

Lloyd D Simpson

Notes on Thomas Jefferson

ISBN/EAN: 9783337397357

Printed in Europe, USA, Canada, Australia, Japan

Cover: Foto ©ninafisch / pixelio.de

More available books at **www.hansebooks.com**

ON

THOMAS JEFFERSON.

BY

A CITIZEN OF MARYLAND.

PHILADELPHIA
SHERMAN & CO., PRINTERS
1885.

CONTENTS.

CHAPTER I.
	PAGE
Introduction, ...	9

CHAPTER II.
Jefferson's Political Animosity, ... 12

CHAPTER III.
His Aversion to Official Life, ... 16

CHAPTER IV.
Jefferson and Presidential Re-eligibility, . . . 21

CHAPTER V.
Jefferson and Religion, ... 29

CHAPTER VI.
The Purchase of Louisiana, ... 40

CHAPTER VII.
Some Tergiversations, Self-contradictions, and Inconsistencies, 44

CHAPTER VIII.
Jefferson's Apprehensions of Monarchy, . . . 56

CHAPTER IX.
Jefferson and The Declaration of Independence, . . . 61

CHAPTER X.
Remarkable Political Theories, ... 72

CHAPTER XI.
Are his "Ana" reliable? 86

CHAPTER XII.
Jefferson as Governor, in Time of War, . . 89

CONTENTS.

CHAPTER XIII.
His Indirectness, ... 102

CHAPTER XIV.
Jefferson and Genét, ... 106

CHAPTER XV.
Jefferson as a Demagogue, ... 114

CHAPTER XVI.
Jefferson and Burr, ... 118

CHAPTER XVII.
Jefferson's Slanders of Hamilton, ... 134

CHAPTER XVIII.
Jefferson and Washington, ... 146

CHAPTER XIX.
Jefferson's Opinion of Riots and Insurrections, . 160

CHAPTER XX.
Some Evidence of his Insincerity, ... 163

CHAPTER XXI.
Jefferson and The French Revolution, ... 177

CHAPTER XXII.
Effects of His Life and Doctrines, ... 179

NOTES ON THOMAS JEFFERSON.

CHAPTER I.

INTRODUCTION.

For obvious reasons, whatever pertains to Thomas Jefferson possesses an interest for all Americans. But he has exercised so prevalent and permanent an influence upon political thought and action in this Republic, that a study of his character must needs prove not only interesting, but profitable to its citizens.

This study is, moreover, invested with a unique attraction by the fact that the character and career of no other prominent person of our Revolutionary era, have elicited such conflicting opinions as the character and career of Jefferson. On the one hand, he has been eulogized as a wise statesman, a man of extraordinary erudition—a profound philosopher. On the other, his statesmanship has been ridiculed, his learning pronounced limited as well as superficial, and his philosophy branded as empirical. Thousands admire and love him because they are convinced that he was a sincere friend of political equality; many assert that he was a demagogue, feigning affection for the people, in order that he might use them for promoting his own aggrandizement. Some think he was happiest in retirement—that he accepted only such honors as were thrust upon him—and those reluctantly; others are persuaded that he was tormented by a consuming ambition,—that he thirsted for preferment, and was not very scrupulous as to the means which he used to obtain it. Some regard him as a simpleminded, ingenuous man; others characterize him as supple and crafty, capable of making himself "all things to all men," in order to accomplish his selfish purposes. Some describe him as gentle and amiable; others declare that he was capable of intense malignity. One extols him as exemplary in his private walk and conversation; another offers to prove that he stooped to repulsive infractions of the law of chastity.

This conflict of opinion, it is believed, results mainly from three causes: 1. Mr. Jefferson was the leader of a political party, at a time when party spirit was violent. His partisans concealed his faults, magnified his merits, and ascribed to him virtues that he did not possess. His political opponents, in their turn, decried him, exaggerating the defects of his nature, and charging him with ignoble actions upon insufficient evidence. 2. He held little direct communication with the people; while it was commonly understood that he was warmly attached to popular government, his views on specific measures of public policy, or his opinion respecting the doctrines held by any statesman were generally expressed, at first, only to a few trusted friends, whose province it was to consider them, and if they were approved, make them known to others. Some of these views and opinions were not communicated to the multitude. Some that were transmitted to the people were mutilated in their transmission: others, so transmitted, were distorted or colored by the personal theories or prejudices of those to whom they were originally imparted. 3. He not infrequently employed ambiguous forms of expression.

The publication, in 1853, of Jefferson's confidential correspondence, his *Ana* and other productions of his, not before given to the world, has furnished all who will use them with data sufficient for forming a correct judgment concerning him and his whole career. No attempt to perform a work so important and extensive has been made in the following notes; but it is hoped that they will throw light on some of his peculiar doctrines, and illustrate some traits of his character, that heretofore have been either too little known, or too much disregarded.

CHAPTER II.

JEFFERSON'S POLITICAL ANIMOSITY.

Jefferson, though a "mild-mannered man," frequently employed acrimonious language respecting those who differed from him politically. In his letter to Mr. Madison, dated December 28th, 1794, he styled the Senate "the Augean stable;" he designated the majority of that body as "his opponents," as "monocrats;" he declared that the Cincinnati were "lowering over the Constitution eternally;" he characterized the excise law of 1791 as "an infernal law;" he said the Government was "patient of the kicks and scoffs of our enemies," but rose "at a feather against our friends," to wit, the whiskey insurrectionists of Pennsylvania. The epithet "anglo-men," he frequently applies to the Federalists. He alludes to "the corrupt squadron" of Congress, "debauched" by the secretary of the Treasury. He declared that Hamilton believed in a monarchy "bottomed on corruption,"—that the public funds were "a contrivance invented for the purposes of corruption." His letter of March 29th, 1801, to Elbridge Gerry, contains numerous vindictive passages, in some of which his bitterness is enveloped in circumlocution—in others, it is but too clearly expressed. We cite some of them. "We may now say that the United States, southwardly from New York, are as unanimous in the principles of '76 as they were in '76. The only difference is, that the leaders who remain behind are more numerous and bolder than the apostles of toryism in 1776. The reason is that we are now justly more tolerant than we could safely have been then." (Mark how ingeniously he endeavors to place upon prominent Federalists the stigma of toryism.) "A coalition of sentiments is not for the interest of the printers; they, like the clergy, live by the zeal they can kindle, and the schisms they can create." "The mild and simple principles of the Christian philosophy would produce too much calm, too much regularity of good, to extract from its disciples a support for a numerous priesthood, were they not to sophisticate it, ramify it, split it into hairs, and twist its texts till they cover the divine morality of its author with mysteries, and require a priesthood to explain them." "Your part of the Union, though as absolutely republican as ours, has drunk deeper of the delusion" (opposition to republicanism)..... "The ægis of government, and the temples of religion and of justice, have all been prostituted there, to toll us back to the times when we burnt witches. The people will support you, notwithstanding the howlings of the ravenous crew from whose jaws they are escaping." According to Jefferson, those opposed to Republicanism were "apostates," whose heads had been "shorn by the Harlot of England:"—"a faction of monocrats:"—the friends of Washington were "the satellites and sycophants" about the President—the publications and newspapers of the Federalists were "The slanderous chronicles of Federalism"—the supporters of Hamilton were "votaries to the treasury," "the stockjobbing herd,"—and the $20,000,000 of stock issued on the assumption of the state debts was "a pabulum thrown in" to this "stock-jobbing herd;"—they who favored the assumption of the debts by the General Government and the funding of the debts thus assumed, together with the national debt, were "gamblers in these scenes;" the Federalists of Massachusetts were "venal traitors." Jefferson wrote that Hamilton's "career from the moment history could stoop to notice him," was "a tissue of machinations against the liberty of a country, which had not only received and fed him, but heaped its honors on his head"—that "the more debt Hamilton could rake up, the more plunder for his mercenaries." This curious paragraph occurs in one of his letters: "*Washington naked would have been sanctimoniously reverenced*, but enveloped in the rags of royalty, they can hardly be torn off without laceration." His wrath against those opposed to democracy waxed so hot, that he found no English words adequate to its expression—he must needs resort to the Greek: he calls the advocates of a strong government," "*Energumenoi* of royalism." It is submitted that a man who could name his opponents "energumenoi," must have been possessed by a fury of no common order. Had Jefferson applied this fearful epithet to Hamilton and Adams in their hearing, he might have produced upon them the same effect that Daniel O'Connell did upon the Billingsgate woman, when he styled her a parallelopipedon. In a letter dated August 14th, 1811, and addressed to General Dearborn of Massachusetts, Jefferson applauds Elbridge Gerry, then the recently elected governor of that state, for removing Federalists from office, commending the governor "for the rasping with which he rubbed down his bed of traitors." "Let them have justice," he adds, " and protection from violence, but no favor. Powers and pre-eminences conferred on them are *daggers put into the hands of assassins, to be plunged in our bosoms the moment the thrust can go home to the heart.*" He further expresses to the general his apprehension that the Federalists, if they regain power, will resort to deportation and the guillotine. The actions and expressions of those engaged in a violent political contest should not be judged too harshly, but this letter written from the seclusion of Monticello, long after Jefferson had ceased all personal participation in the strife of contending parties, is a melancholy exhibition of political venom.

CHAPTER III.

HIS AVERSION TO OFFICIAL LIFE.

In 1781, shortly after he resigned the governorship of Virginia, deeply chagrined by the strictures upon his management of affairs, during the invasions of Arnold and General Tarleton, Jefferson wrote to a friend that "every fibre of his political ambition was eradicated," and that he would never return to public life. The next year, he accepted the position of a commissioner to treat for peace with Great Britain. He, however, took no part in the negotiations; in fact did not quit the country, a provisional treaty having been signed before he could sail, by the other commissioners already in Europe. In June, 1783, he was chosen a delegate to Congress. In 1784 he was appointed to assist Benjamin Franklin and John Adams in negotiating treaties of commerce with various European States. Shortly after his arrival in Europe, in pursuance of this mission, he was appointed minister at the Court of Versailles. It thus appears that, within a period of less than five years, after declaring his disgust at popular ingratitude and his determination never again to enter public life, he accepted four official positions. Before leaving France, which he did in 1789, he received from Mr. Madison a letter, asking whether he would accept an appointment at home. He replied that he desired retirement; that all his appointments to office had been contrary to his wishes, and that he had resigned the French mission in order "to resume his agricultural pursuits, and the enjoyment of total seclusion and rest." He reached Monticello on December 23d, 1789. On March 1st, 1790, he again quitted his home for the purpose of assuming the office of Secretary of State under Washington, having pursued agriculture and enjoyed seclusion and rest for two months and eight days. He held that position till the expiration of Washington's first term, and took the same place under Washington's second administration. In his letter of December 31st, 1793, announcing to the President his resignation of office, Jefferson writes, "My propensity to retirement is becoming daily more and more irresistible." On December 28th, 1794, he writes Mr. Madison, "I would not give up my own retirement for the empire of the universe." In his letter to Mr. Madison of April 27th, 1795, he repeats his determination to remain in private life, assigning as reasons therefor, "My health is entirely broken down, . . . my age requires that I should place my affairs in a clear state, . . . and above all, the delights I feel in the society of my family and in agricultural pursuits;" he assures Mr. Madison that the writer is not to be reasoned out of his resolution, and apparently, with the view of preventing all attempts in that direction, he adds, "*The question is forever closed with me.*"

On June 19th, 1796, he advised General Washington that he was devoting himself to the cultivation of "lucerne, pease and potatoes," and took no concern in politics and public measures. In October of the same year, Mr. Jefferson, notwithstanding his lack of interest in politics, was chosen Vice-President of the United States. He doubtless declined the proffered dignity. They who entertain that idea have a very erroneous conception of Mr. Jefferson's character. He was not the man to disregard the call of his country. A few weeks after the news of his election was confirmed, he left Monticello, casting, we may well believe, "many a longing, lingering look behind," upon his "lucerne, pease and potatoes," and journeyed to Philadelphia, then the seat of the Federal Government, where he was inducted into the office of Vice-President. While still holding this position, the Presidential election of 1800 took place. When the electoral votes were counted, it appeared that Mr. Jefferson and Aaron Burr had received the same number. There was, consequently, no choice by the Electoral College, and the duty of choosing a President was devolved upon the House of Representatives. Into the long and bitter contest that ensued, Mr. Jefferson warmly entered, seemingly forgetful of the charms of retirement in his zeal for the success of the great party with which he was now identified.

The contest, as is well known, resulted in the choice of "the sage of Monticello," who thereupon took up his residence in the White House. In the spring of 1804, he communicated to Mr. Page the fact that he was looking forward to "domestic comfort," at the expiration of his official term. But, re-elected President in the autumn of that year, his desire to promote the welfare of his fellow-citizens, from whom he could withhold nothing in his power to grant, impelled him again to postpone the coveted enjoyment of domestic comfort. Yet the old feeling was strong upon him. Though crowned with honors and enshrined in the hearts of his countrymen, he yearned for the seclusion of his rural home. That this is true, we know from a letter written shortly after his re-election to Elbridge Gerry. In it the President states that his great desire had "been to retire at the end of the present term to a life of tranquility, and it was my decided purpose when I entered into office." It thus appears that he not only desired, but had purposed retirement. Twice in the letter he expresses the ever-recurring wish "to enjoy my family, my farm and my books." He did not, however, selfishly resign, as many men with his intense longing for retirement, would have done. He conceived that the exigencies of the time demanded his continuance "at the helm," and rightly concluding that personal feelings must be disregarded when national interests are at stake, he bore, without a murmur, four years longer, his painful separation from the beloved objects above mentioned.

The example of Mr. Jefferson in this regard is commended to the youth of the country. His devotion to public duty was as rare as it was admirable. Quite unfitted, as he intimates, to brave the storms which all, who then embarked on the sea of American politics, would inevitably encounter, he nevertheless, again and again, at the call of his country, tried that tempestuous sea. Though feeling an aversion to the duties of office so strong, that he characterizes the discharge of some of them as a "martyrdom," he twelve times yielded to the importunities of the people when they demanded his services. Delighting in agricultural pursuits, ever longing for the quiet and seclusion of his pleasant home; harassed by a propensity for retirement, which, as he declared, became at times irresistible; so profoundly interested in "lucerne, pease and potatoes," that neither the lapse of time, nor protracted absence, nor affairs of state, caused him to forget those useful vegetables, he yet remained in public life, with brief intervals, for a period of forty years. Behold in Jefferson a man whose strong patriotism subdued and held in bondage his cherished aims and desires. The envious or the hostile might indeed accuse him of vacillation, or hint at insincerity, because he several times accepted office after having twice expressed his fixed determination never again to do so, but such frivolous charges and insinuations were unheard or unheeded, so absorbed was he in the great work of saving our republican institutions from the assaults of the Federalists.

CHAPTER IV.

JEFFERSON AND PRESIDENTIAL RE-ELIGIBILITY.

On November 3d, 1787, Mr. Jefferson, then in Paris, in a letter to John Adams, expresses strong disapprobation of the re-eligibility of the President, permitted by the new Constitution. He writes: " Once in office and possessing the military force of the Union, . . he would not be easily dethroned, even if the people could be induced to withdraw their votes from him." . . " I wish at the end of the four years they had made him forever ineligible a second time." In March, 1789, he writes to F. Hopkinson: "Since the thing (Constitution) has been established, I would wish it not to be altered during the life of our great leader, who alone, by the authority of his name and the confidence reposed in his perfect integrity, is fully qualified to put the new Government so under way as to secure it against the efforts of opposition," but hopes the Constitution will be corrected the moment " we can no longer have the same name at the helm." We can well understand how the pre-eminent services rendered to his country by Washington might induce Mr. Jefferson to waive his opposition to re-eligibility in the case of that "great leader," but in view of his letter to Mr. Adams, his willingness to have Washington continuously re-elected for life, is somewhat surprising. It has not escaped observation that when he expressed this willingness, Washington was President-elect, that Jefferson was then anxious to be re-called from France, that he soon returned to the United

States, and that in less than two months after reaching home, he had received and accepted the appointment of Secretary of State. It will be noted, that in the first letter the writer's estimate of the President's power is very different from the estimate placed upon it in the second. In the former, he apprehended that the Chief Executive will with difficulty be "dethroned, even if the people withdraw their votes from him." In the latter, he doubts whether any President save Washington can sustain the new Government until it gets well under way. In November, 1787, he fears the powers and privileges conferred by the Constitution upon the President will enable whoever is chosen, to perpetuate his authority in defiance of law and the will of the people. In March, 1789, he thinks that during the early days of the Republic, there will probably be but one man in the nation strong enough to retain the office of President until the expiration of his constitutional term. The year 1807 witnessed a further change in his views, either as to the constitutional powers of the President, or as to the influence of Washington. We quote from Mr. Jefferson's notes in the fifth volume of Marshall's *Life of Washington*, published in that year: "I am satisfied that Washington had no wish to perpetuate his authority; but he who supposes it was practicable, had he wished it, knows nothing of the spirit of America." Here, far from being apprehensive of the Chief Magistrate's power to perpetuate his authority beyond his lawful term of office, Jefferson scouts the idea that even "our great leader," with his unparalleled popularity and the weight of his great name, could have done so.

We have mentioned Jefferson's hope respecting the correction of the Constitution. The earnestness with which that hope was expressed warranted the expectation that he who expressed it would immediately, upon Washington's retirement, endeavor to effect the correction. But, so far as known, he made no movement in that direction. Had rising visions of his own first and second terms in the new executive mansion, to be erected on the banks of the Potomac, already concealed from his view the rocks and shoals of re-eligibility? The world will never know; but neither then, nor at any subsequent time, did his hope ripen into action. He lived many years after Washington quitted office; he had ample leisure; he obtained extraordinary influence over his fellow-countrymen; he suggested and aided to secure the adoption of several amendments of the Constitution, but sank into the grave without so much as publicly proposing the amendment, deemed by him so vitally important that he hoped it would be made the moment Washington abandoned the helm. Not only did he make no attempt to secure that amendment, which might indeed have been a difficult task, but he deliberately violated the doctrine that he had early enunciated and strongly advocated—he himself accepted a re-election. Apparently conscious that some explanation of this action was due to those familiar with his oft-expressed opinion, he writes, "I sincerely regret that the unbounded calumnies of the Federal party have obliged me to throw myself on the verdict of my country for trial." The excuse here offered for his dereliction seems worse than the fault. He seeks to justify his departure from his own standard of good government by a consideration wholly personal. By his own admission, he inconsistently consented to a re-election, not because the public welfare demanded it, or because the importunities of his friends overcame his scruples, but for the weighty reason that his political opponents calumniated him. One of his biographers, commenting upon this proceeding, writes,

"How much of real glory he lost by missing this opportunity of putting the seal of sincerity and the test of consistency on his original professions, can only be estimated by a full consideration of the difficulty attending the sacrifice of ambition to principle." Having transgressed himself, he could hardly attempt to check the friends who followed his example. He witnessed the re-election and inauguration of Mr. Madison and of Mr. Monroe without a word of disapprobation. On December 10th, 1807, he declined a third election, stating his main reason therefor as follows: " I should unwillingly be the person who, disregarding the sound precedent set by an illustrious predecessor, should furnish the first example of prolongation beyond the second term of office."

On September 20th, 1813, he writes " I prefer the Presidential term of four years to that of seven years, which I at first suggested, annexing to it, however, ineligibility for ever after, and I wish it were now annexed to the second quadrennial election of President." In his autobiography, dated January 6th, 1821, we find him preferring to a seven years term "the present practice of allowing a continuance for eight years, to be dropped at half way of the term, making that a period of probation." In his *Ana*, under the year 1792, there is a passage, which by implication, favors a term of seven years, with ineligibility for seven years thereafter.

To recapitulate: Mr. Jefferson originally suggested that presidential incumbency should be limited to a single term of seven years. He next favored a single term of four years.

Scarcely fifteen months had elapsed, when he desired Washington's continuous re-election during life, but hoped the provision for a single term of four years would be incorporated in the Constitution, as soon as practicable after

Washington's retirement. In 1792, he favors a term of seven years, to be followed by a seven years interval of ineligibility. His next known opinion on the subject, is found in the letters declining a third election. In these he makes no mention of the evils of re-eligibility, indirectly favors two successive terms of four years each, mildly disapproves three successive elections, and says nothing of eligibility after an interval. In 1813, bidding a final adieu to his first choice—a seven years term, he prefers a presidential term of four years and wishes ineligibility "annexed to the second quadrennial election," by a change in the fundamental law. Finally, in 1821, having abandoned, as it seems, either the wish or the hope of securing such an amendment of the Constitution as he had suggested, he sets the seal of his approbation upon the practice of "allowing a continuance for eight years, with a liability to be dropped at half-way of the term"—as he curiously expresses it. Here we have a *menu* of opinion's so varied as to suit all tastes. How well Mr. Jefferson's actions tallied with his professed opinions on the question of re-eligibility, is written in the annals of the nation. He, as has been intimated, expressed fears that re-eligibility would prove detrimental to the country. Should his worst apprehensions in regard to its evil effects be realized, should the presidency be transformed by re-eligibility into an office for life, as he asserted it would be, upon himself must rest the chief, if not the sole responsibility for this and all other ills springing from the same source. For, although the re-election of the president is theoretically permitted by the Constitution, it became an actuality through the agency of Mr. Jefferson and those whose political movements he controlled. The acceptance, in immediate succession, of a second term by Jefferson, Madison, and Monroe, firmly established the practice of re-electing a president, before the expiration of his first term. It may be safely assumed that neither Mr. Madison nor Mr. Monroe would have consented to a re-election had Mr. Jefferson refused it, and advised them to follow his example, for in matters political, he was their "guide, philosopher, and friend." Nor can the second election of Washington be pleaded as a precedent, because his acceptance thereof was urged in such a manner and for such reasons that he could scarcely refuse, how strong soever his reluctance; and the condition of affairs was, at the time, quite exceptional. On the other hand, should re-eligibility continue as harmless as it has shown itself to be, during the past century, the failure of Mr. Jefferson's repeated prognostications of its mischievous results must greatly diminish our estimate of his political sagacity. But whether re-eligibility yield good or evil fruits, whether the forebodings of Mr. Jefferson were groundless or not, his own letters and the pages of history clearly show that he gave his example and his great influence in support of a governmental principle, which he had often reprobated as pernicious, so pernicious that he assured a friend it "would produce cruel distress in our country."

Mr. Jefferson has been much commended for refusing to be President for more than two terms. Let us briefly examine the history and incidents of this refusal.

1. When he styles Washington's retirement at the expiration of his second term a "sound precedent," he indirectly admits the propriety of a second term; this admission, and his own acceptance of a re-election, while in the office of President, may be fairly regarded as an abandonment of his original opinion on the question of Presidential re-eligibility—which position was that the Executive should "forever be ineligible a second time." When an abandon-

ment of one's professed convictions secures continued honor and emoluments, it is scarcely a ground for commendation.

2. Mr. Jefferson's disapproval of a third term is not very strongly expressed. His language is: "I should unwillingly be the person who . . . should furnish the first example of a prolongation." Observe, he does not absolutely refuse a third election—not at all. He but declares his reluctance to be the first person who should disregard the precedent set by Washington. He indicates no calamities that would likely result from a third term. He does not even state his own opinion on the subject.

3. He adduces as additional reasons for declining, the burdens and infirmities of increasing years, and his strong desire to enjoy the repose of private life.

4. The evils to be apprehended from the re-eligibility of an actual incumbent are the same whether re-eligible for one or for two terms. "Once in office and possessed of the military force of the Union, he would not be easily dethroned," are Mr. Jefferson's own words. The danger of re-eligibility, if there be any such danger, is that the incumbent will employ his immense patronage and the military forces, of which he is commander-in-chief, to secure his re-election. This danger manifestly begins as soon as he has grasped the reins of power.

5. The address of the Vermont Legislature, in which Mr. Jefferson is asked to serve a third term, was dated November 5th, 1806, and was duly received. His reply thereto, from which we have quoted, stating his unwillingness, was written December 10th, 1807, more than a year afterwards. In the interim, he had received and answered a communication from the Vermont Legislature upon another subject. Considering this fact, his guarded lan-

guage, and his delay in replying to the address, we may not uncharitably suppose that when he received the same, he had not decided to retire at the expiration of the current term; that for some time after the address reached him he was not unwilling to be re-elected; that he was not impelled to refuse by fears that a third term would imperil our free institutions; that before determining to retire he had well pondered the advantages and disadvantages of the movement, as well as carefully considered the probabilities of success in the ensuing Presidential campaign. Indeed, a gentleman of distinction, formerly United States Senator, who has given the subject attention, believes that Mr. Jefferson's letter in answer to the address was not penned until, by diligent inquiry, he had satisfied himself that his re-election was by no means certain. This belief derives some support from the fact, that about the time he communicated to the Vermont Legislature his determination not to accept a third term, he wrote several communications of like tenor to other parties.

CHAPTER V.

JEFFERSON AND RELIGION.

Mr. Jefferson's skepticism was known to some and suspected by many of his contemporaries, but the nature and scope of that skepticism were only matters of conjecture until the publication of his private correspondence. This correspondence, and the investigations which resulted from its being made public seem to show that he was a radical, uncompromising, and sometimes bitter infidel; that he had little sympathy, and perhaps less respect for any form of religious faith.

He was the friendly associate of scoffers and unbelievers, both native and foreign born, among whom may be mentioned the scurrilous Paine, Condorcet, Cabanis, General Dearborn and Mr. Freneau. The *National Gazette*, his personal and political organ, almost entirely under his control, vilified clergymen and mocked at religion.

In his letters, he assails Presbyterianism, characterizes "the five points of Calvin" as "blasphemous absurdity," and rails at the theology of the great Genevan doctor as follows: "It would be more pardonable to believe in no God, than to blaspheme him by the atrocious attributes of Calvin." He styles Presbyterians the "loyalists of our country." He madly compares them to the Jesuits, and in a paroxysm of folly, he pronounces Calvin an atheist.

He writes: "The metaphysical absurdities of Athanasius, of Loyola, and of Calvin are mere relapses into polytheism, differing from Paganism only in being more unintelligible."

He vehemently attacks Trinitarians and the doctrine of the Trinity. In one letter, he thus expresses himself: "I would as soon undertake to bring the crazy skulls of Bedlam to sound understanding, as to inculcate reason into that of an Athanasian;" in another to James Smith, is found the following: "Nor was the unity of the Supreme Being ousted from the Christian creed by the force of reason, but by the sword of civil government, wielded at the will of the fanatic Athanasius.* The hocus-pocus phantasm of a God, like another Cerberus, with one body and three heads, had its birth and growth in the blood of thousands and thousands of martyrs." They, who witnessed only the calm amenity that Jefferson almost invariably displayed to those who casually met him, little suspected that within his bosom there lurked such venom. In the same letter, written December 8th, 1822, he says: "I confidently expect that the present generation will see Unitarianism become the general religion of the United States."

While discrediting all the Holy Scriptures, he singles out certain portions and statements found in them as specially objectionable. In a letter dated January 17th, 1825, to General Smith, he considers the Apocalypse "*merely as the ravings of a maniac*—no more worthy or capable of explanation than the incoherent cries of our nightly dreams." In that letter, or in one written about the same time, he predicts "The day will come when the mystical generation of Jesus in the womb of a virgin, by the Supreme Being as his father, will be classed with the generation of Minerva in the brain of Jupiter." Having branded the venerable exile of Patmos as a maniac, he

---

* The sword of civil government was wielded not for Athanasius, but against him. He was four times banished from Alexandria, and once saved himself from violence by voluntary exile.

seeks to disparage the Epistles, labors and preaching of St. Paul, by reprobating him as the "*Coryphaeus of the band of dupes and robbers,*" who endeavored to propagate impostures concerning Christ. We think no one, believer or infidel, except Jefferson, has ever imputed stupidity and insincerity to the great Apostle of the Gentiles. In his famous letter to Dr. Rush respecting religious beliefs, he attempts to impeach the credibility of the four Gospels by alleging, that they who undertook to preserve the doctrines of Christ "wrote from memory, and not till long after the transactions had passed;" that Jesus perished at the age of thirty-three, before he had completed his system; that "the doctrines which he really delivered were defective as a whole, and fragments only of what he did deliver have come to us mutilated, misstated and often unintelligible." Yet, with pretended zeal for what he is pleased to term the "simple" doctrines of Christ, he writes to Timothy Pickering: "The religion-builders have so distorted and deformed the doctrines of Jesus—so muffled them in mysticisms, fancies and falsehoods; have caricatured them into forms so monstrous and inconceivable as to shock reasonable thinkers, to revolt them against the whole, and drive them rashly to pronounce its founder an impostor."

If the statements respecting the doctrines of Christ, made in the letter to Dr. Rush, are correct, the charges found in the letter to Mr. Pickering cannot be sustained. If we have only mutilated, misstated, and unintelligible fragments of what Jesus delivered, it is manifestly impossible for "us" to know what are the doctrines really taught by the Son of Mary, and consequently impossible to determine whether they have or have not been "distorted and deformed." It is evident that Jefferson's antipathy to "religion-builders" induced him to make absurd and contradictory allegations against them, and the foundations of their faith. Equally absurd, and more ridiculous, when contrasted with the citations from the Rush letter, is a certain declaration of Jefferson concerning his own religious views. It runs thus: "It is not to be understood that I am with Christ in *all* his doctrines. I am a materialist. He takes the side of spiritualism." The self-esteem here apparent, it may be remarked, is quite Jeffersonian.

In a letter to his nephew, Peter Carr, dated August 10th, 1787, Jefferson thus instructs his young relative: "Your own reason is the only oracle given you by Heaven, and you are answerable, not for the rightness, but uprightness of its decision. Read the Bible, then, as you would Livy or Tacitus. . . . The New Testament is a history of a personage called Jesus. Keep in your eye the opposite pretensions, (1) of those who say he was begotten by God, born of a virgin, suspended and reversed the laws of nature at will, and ascended bodily to Heaven; and, (2) of those who say he was a man of illegitimate birth, of a benevolent heart, and enthusiastic mind, who set out without pretensions to divinity, ended in believing them, and was punished capitally for sedition. . . . Question with boldness even the existence of a God; because, if there be one, he must more approve of the homage of reason than that of blindfolded fear. Do not be frightened from this inquiry by any fear of consequences. If it ends in the belief that there is no God, you will find incitements to virtue in the comfort and pleasantness you feel in its exercise, and in the love of others which it will procure you. If you find reason to believe that there is a God, a consciousness that you are acting under his eye, and that he approves you, will be a vast additional incitement."

From contempt for the oracles of Christianity and their

authors, to the abuse of its divine founder the transition is easy. It is, therefore, not surprising to find Jefferson, in a letter to Dr. Rush, charging the Saviour with "evasions, sophisms, misconstructions, and misapplications of scraps of the prophets." In keeping with this, is his reply to his Italian friend (Mazzei), who called his attention to the dilapidated condition of a church in Virginia. "It is good enough," observed Jefferson, "for one who was born in a manger."

He believed the prevalent forms of the Christian religion to be dangerous to the Republic. On November 2d, 1822, he wrote to Dr. Cooper: " The atmosphere of our country is unquestionably charged with a threatening cloud of fanaticism,—lighter in some places, denser in others, but too heavy in all." His friend, General Dearborn, of Massachusetts, whom he appointed Secretary of War, declared that so long as our Christian temples stood "we could not hope for good order or good government."

Jefferson traduced ministers and members of Christian churches. Writing to the Dr. Cooper above mentioned, he thus ridicules some pious women of his own State: "In our Richmond there is much fanaticism, but chiefly among the women. They have their night meetings and praying parties, where, attended by their priests, and sometimes by a henpecked husband, they pour forth the effusions of their love to Jesus, in terms as amatory and carnal as their modesty would permit them to use to a mere earthly lover." But his hottest indignation is reserved for the ministers. His wrath against these "impious dogmatists," these "false shepherds," these "mere usurpers of the Christian name," transports him beyond the bounds of reason and decorum. "My opinion is," he writes, "that there would never have been an infidel if there had never been a priest." He fairly raves at the "Parishes, the Ogdens," and other clergymen of New England, whom he styles "Marats, Dantons, and Robespieres." Finally, in a letter to Dr. Rush, he includes all clergymen in one sweeping denunciation, by declaring that "*the riddle of all priesthoods is solved in four words —'Ubi panis, ibi Deus.'*" When it is remembered that in the Christian ministry, from the date of its institution to the time of Jefferson, there were always men of great intellect, sound reason, disinterested benevolence, and unsullied character, wholly devoted to the service of their Heavenly King, and the benefaction of their fellow-men, and that Jefferson could not have been ignorant of this thing, his declaration just above quoted must be pronounced not only untrue, but wilfully malicious. Here, as in his attitude towards Saint Paul, he stands alone. Not even the "grinning skeleton" of France, in his fiercest onslaughts upon the founder of Christianity, ventured to stigmatize as mercenary hypocrites the pure and holy men, who have sacrificed at her altars.

In further illustration of Mr. Jefferson's religious opinions, it may be stated that in founding the University of Virginia, of which he claimed to be the "father," no provision was made for a school, or even a professorship of divinity; that he classed the various forms of Christian belief under the one head of "fanaticism;" that he characterized them all, Quakerism and Unitarianism excepted, as "dreams of the night;" that he attempted to maintain that Christianity was not a part of the Common Law of England, in the face of a line of judicial decisions, unbroken, we believe, down to the time at which he wrote, and in opposition to Lord Keeper Finch, Wingate, Shepherd, author of the Touchstone, Lord Hale, Wood, Blackstone, Lord Mansfield, and other eminent jurists.

Was Jefferson an atheist? In order to show his belief in a Supreme Being, his best biographer, Mr. Randall, quotes from his inaugural addresses and his messages, certain phrases wherein he invokes the Deity. But these were public documents, and it need not be said to those, who have impartially studied the life and character of Jefferson, that his public utterances are by no means conclusive evidence of his real opinions. If the maxim "*noscitur a sociis*" be applied to him, it raises a presumption of his atheism. Freneau, his protegé, eulogist, and champion flouted a belief in Providence. His cherished friend, General Dearborn, as stated above, desired the demolition of the temples of God. His French friend, Cabanis, taught that "the moral affections and intellectual faculties reside in the nerves;" that there is no distinction between the physical and the moral nature, for "the moral faculties have their origin in the physical." In other words, man is like the beasts that perish; when the physical body dies all is dead—there is no immortality—no future. Condorcet, another and more intimate French friend, declared that "*to deny God is the sublime of philosophy.*" Jefferson's writings strengthens the presumption raised by his associates. In his notes on Virginia, he says "It does me no harm for my neighbor to say there are twenty Gods or no God; it does not break my bones." In one of the passages cited from his letter to his nephew, he intimates that a belief in God is of little importance, since they who do not believe will find other incentives to virtue. And the passage, "Question with boldness even the existence of a God, because if there be one," etc., may be fairly interpreted to imply a doubt, if not a disbelief in such existence. He has not, we think, left on record any clear expression of his trust in an overruling Providence. His flippant use of such phrases as "by the God that made me" will scarcely be adduced as evidence of his faith in a personal Deity. During his last hours, he declined all religious converse, and gave no sign of a belief in a future state. Mr. Parton, in his labored eulogy, facetiously styled a life of Jefferson, says "his religion was the supreme decency, the highest etiquette, with the addition of bell-ringing and merry Christmas." If this description of his religion by one of his warmest admirers be correct, Jefferson was certainly an atheist.

Let us now turn for a moment from this melange of conceit, malevolence, and blasphemy to the life and writings of Benjamin Franklin, a skeptic indeed, but one whose skepticism we can respect, if not approve. He accords to Christianity the deference due to a religion that has claims to a superhuman origin, that numbers among its votaries many of the wisest and best of our fellow-creatures, that, having for eighteen hundred years withstood the assaults of its enemies, is now enshrined in the hearts of millions. In November 1764, when about to depart for Europe, he wrote to his daughter, "Go constantly to church, no matter who preaches; I wish you would never miss the prayer-days." He advised Paine to burn the Age of Reason, before it was seen by any one else;—"not to unchain the tiger." "If," added he, "men are so wicked with religion, what would they be without it?" He publicly announced the belief that "God governs in the affairs of men." He proposed prayer in the Constitutional Convention. Though he denied the divinity of Jesus, he obeyed his precepts. He neither derided nor denounced professing Christians, lay or clerical. It would have been impossible for him to apply to Saint Paul the epithets "dupe and robber," or to charge all ministers of religion with insincerity. He endeavored to live and die as Christians pray that they may live and die, "in perfect charity with all men." What a contrast is here between the real philosopher, Benjamin Franklin, and the pseudo sage of Monticello!

Mr. Randall informs us that Jefferson contributed to the support of the Protestant Episcopal Church, regularly attended the same, made the responses in the services, and was married and buried by its forms. Mr. Randall, no doubt, wishes his readers to infer from these facts that Jefferson's infidelity was not very pronounced; that he had not the strong aversion to religion, that his enemies imputed to him. And such inferences are indeed warranted by these facts, standing alone; but their importance can only be determined by considering them in the light of Mr. Jefferson's declarations, and of all his other acts. He must have despised the clergymen who officiated at the church which he attended, since all clergymen were included in his general denunciation of them. It is hard to believe that he respected one of those religions that he asserted to be fanaticisms. It is most improbable that he cherished friendly feelings for the Episcopal, as distinguished from other Christian churches, for he had been her most active opponent in the contest which resulted in the overthrow of her supremacy and the loss of her property in Virginia. It is then reasonable to conclude that his subsequent attendance at her service was prompted by other than religious motives. He was probably, somewhat influenced in this action by the wishes of his family, by the "supreme decency" mentioned by Mr. Parton, and by a desire to avoid offending the prejudices of his neighbors. But there must have been an incentive stronger than any of these, to induce him not only to endure, but to aid that for which he had expressed emphatic contempt, and that incentive may be found in his political opinions and career. Mr. Jefferson was a Democrat; he professed strong confidence in the purity and wisdom of the masses of the people. He knew full well that a great majority of them favored the Christian religion, and in order to win and retain their support, which was essential to secure the triumph of himself and his party, he must exhibit some regard for Christian churches and their ordinances. He therefore not only abstained from any overt attack upon religion, but attended the Episcopal Church and contributed to its maintenance.

It may have been not his religious convictions or the voice of conscience, but the voice of the people, regarded by Jefferson as the voice of God, that summoned him to the temples of the Most High. If he attended church services in early life, it was possibly because others did so, or because he hoped to promote thereby his own advancement. His attendance, in later years, may have resulted from habit, from a desire to disprove the allegations of his enemies as to his infidelity, or above all, from a wish to perpetuate the ascendancy of his party and of his party associates. While manifesting this outward deference to religion, he was writing to his friends private letters, filled with "hatred, malice and all uncharitableness" towards Christians and the prevalent forms of Christian faith. His course in this matter brings out in strong relief his duplicity, the great blemish in his character. In a number of his letters derogatory to Christians, are found injunctions of secrecy. Thus, while charging clergymen with imposture, he was himself something very like an impostor. While branding others as fanatics, he was himself a bigot. This review of Jefferson's opinions and treatment of religious subjects, may be fitly concluded by citing his revolting allusion to Heaven, penned at Paris, September 30th, 1785, and found in his works, vol. 1, page 327. It is as follows:

"Voltaire's description of France is a true picture of that country, to which they say we shall pass hereafter, and where we are to see God and his angels in splendor, and crowds of the damned trampled under their feet."

CHAPTER VI.

THE PURCHASE OF LOUISIANA.

Mr. Jefferson has been lauded for the acquisition of Louisiana. The purchase of that territory has certainly been most advantageous to the United States, but it may be doubted whether Jefferson deserves much commendation for the part he took in the transaction. It is true he favored and aided the acquisition, but he believed it to be unconstitutional. This fact is established beyond all question by his letters to Mr. Madison, to Levi Lincoln, to W. C. Nicholas, and to Mr. Breckenridge, in regard to the newly-acquired territory. Writing to the gentleman last mentioned, August 12th, 1803, he says: "The Constitution made no provision for our holding foreign territory, still less for incorporating foreign territory into our Union. The Executive in seizing the fugitive occurrence, which so much advances the good of their country, have done an act beyond the Constitution." This is sufficiently explicit. Other citations would be superfluous. Mr. Nicholas endeavored to convince Jefferson that the purchase was constitutional, but he refused to be convinced, and insisted that he had violated the Constitution. He justified his unlawful action by adverting to the great benefits likely to result from it, and urged members of Congress to vote the necessary appropriation for the same reason. He said the unconstitutional purchase of Louisiana might be compared to the illegal investment of his ward's money by a guardian, when such investment was clearly advantageous to the former. When the ward attained his majority, the guardian could say to him: "This purchase was undoubtedly illegal. You have a right to repudiate it and ruin me, but I was prompted to make it by my desire to benefit you." Jefferson was confident the people would endorse the unauthorized acquisition, by voting an amendment to the Constitution. He prepared several drafts of what he deemed a suitable amendment, and submitted them to some of his friends. In a letter to Levi Lincoln he writes: "I quote this (the amendment proposed), observing that the less that is said about any constitutional difficulty the better, and that it will be desirable for Congress to do what is necessary in silence." He appears to have had two reasons for this extraordinary injunction of silence: the fear that his opinion as to the unconstitutionality of the measure might induce some members of Congress to vote against it, and the fear that France, upon learning of constitutional difficulties, might repudiate the contract. In his message to Congress, announcing the purchase, Jefferson made no mention of an amendment for the purpose of rendering it constitutional—no such amendment was ever adopted, or proposed by Congress, or by State legislatures. One can imagine an emergency, in which the Executive might be warranted in disregarding some provision of the Constitution, in order to save the State;—*salus populi, suprema lex*. But Jefferson deliberately did what he admitted to be an unconstitutional act, when neither the existence nor the safety of the Commonwealth was menaced, merely for the purpose of acquiring territory. He, who had repeatedly censured Hamilton, Adams, and even Washington for the exercise of powers the constitutionality of which was but questionable, was guilty of what he deemed a palpable violation of the supreme law. His seeming non-appreciation of the magnitude of his offence is more surprising than the offence itself. Mr. Jefferson's infraction of the Constitution, and his failure to realize the importance of the act will aid us in estimating his respect for that instrument, as well as for laws in general. His comparison of the relations existing between the Federal authorities and the people to those of a guardian and ward, throws light on his notion of the functions of government, and reveals his legal acumen. His belief that the acquisition of Louisiana was repugnant to the Constitution, coupled with his opinion that an amendment would render it constitutional, illustrates his ability to interpret that great charter, and also the profundity of his statesmanship. His injunction of silence, considered with reference to our people and to France, concerns his moral character, and his ready abandonment of the amendment idea may be variously construed.

It will never be known how seriously Jefferson's constitutional difficulties imperilled the success of the negotiations for the purchase of Louisiana. That it was placed in jeopardy by them may be inferred from his own writings. In the letter to Mr. Nicholas he says: "If we give them (the French) the least opening they will declare the treaty void." In other letters, his fear of the injurious effects that a knowledge of his views of the Executive power would produce in France, is apparent. He assigns this as one of the reasons why the treaty should be ratified, and the purchase-money appropriated, with as little debate and as much expedition as possible. Desirous as France was of declaring the treaty void, would she not have done so had she, before its ratification, known that the President believed the Government had no power to make the purchase? There can be no doubt of it. The fact that the power was questioned could scarcely be kept secret for any great length of time, in a country governed as ours then was. Indeed, Jefferson, in referring to a remarkable document received from France by the State Department, seems to intimate that she had an inkling of the constitutional difficulty.

If she had any suspicion of such difficulty, our country was brought to the very verge of a serious calamity by the President's narrow construction of the Constitution. Mr. Jefferson's participation in the Louisiana purchase may be thus summarized. He perceived that the possession of the territory would prove greatly advantageous to the United States, but he was firmly convinced that its acquisition would be a violation of the Constitution. As he had sworn to "preserve, protect, and defend" that instrument, he naturally hesitated. Finding, however, that the popular will demanded the purchase, and that some of his friends deemed the transaction constitutional, he concealed his personal convictions on the subject from the public and from France, urged forward the negotiations, and gave his official sanction to the measure, hoping and believing that it could and would be rendered constitutional by an amendment.

CHAPTER VII.

SOME TERGIVERSATIONS, SELF-CONTRADICTIONS, AND INCONSISTENCIES.

1. On March 15th, 1789, Jefferson wrote: "I know there are some among us who would establish a monarchy, but they are inconsiderable in number and weight of character.... The rising men are all republicans.... *An apostate from republicanism to royalism is impossible.*" In 1793, he entered among his *Ana* the memorandum that we were then "*galloping into a monarchy.*" On April 24th, 1796, he informed Mr. Mazzei by letter, that in place of the "love of republican government" a monarchical party had sprung up in this country; that the party was receiving numerous and important accessions. He thus alludes to the character of the men who had become monarchists: "It would give you a fever were I name to you the *apostates who have gone over*, ... men who were Samsons in the field, and Solomons in the council." He concludes by assuring his friend Mazzei that "our liberty can only be preserved by unremitting labors and perils." Up to the time of his election to the Presidency, he continued to express strong fears lest the government might be converted into a monarchy.

2. On March 15th, 1789, Jefferson, commenting on the recently ratified Constitution, writes: "The executive in our government is not the sole—it is scarcely the principal object of my jealousy. The tyranny of the *legislature* is the most formidable dread of this time, and will be for

many years. That of the executive will come, but it will be at a remote period." As early, however, as 1793, he began to express alarm at the great and increasing power of the executive, and before the close of Washington's second term, he concludes that the President possessed more power than the legislature. (See letter to Madison, June 12th, 1796, and letter to Burr, June 17th, 1797.) At first, he attributed the preponderating influence of the President to the popularity of Washington, but subsequently perceiving that this influence continued after Washington's second term had expired, he became apprehensive that the executive would absorb all the powers of the government. (Letters to Gerry and others in 1797.) In the lapse of time, Jefferson discovered that it was not from Congress, or from the executive, that "we have most to fear," but that the *judiciary* was the arch enemy of our institutions. On Christmas day, 1820, he wrote Thomas Ritchie: "The judiciary of the United States is the subtle corps of sappers and miners constantly working underground to undermine the foundations of our confederate fabric. . . . They will lay all things at their feet." In 1789, he dreads the legislature, and believes the executive will ultimately be dangerous, but not till a remote period. In 1797, he was alarmed lest the executive possess himself of all power; in 1820, he predicts that the judiciary will "lay all things at their feet." His fears as to the powers of the three great departments of the government have proved groundless, his predictions have not been fulfilled, and his calculations in regard to them only reveal the shallowness of his opinions, and his self-contradictions.

3. In a Cabinet opinion, he asserted that the incorporation of a national bank "*sapped the foundations of the Constitution.*" When President, in 1804, he signed a bill

establishing a branch of the National Bank at New Orleans. In 1798, in the famous Kentucky resolutions, he pronounced the law punishing the counterfeiting of national bank notes, "void and of no force," because repugnant to the Constitution. In 1807, he signed a bill to punish as capital offences certain frauds on this bank. Albert Gallatin states that Jefferson favored a recharter of the bank, and suggested that the bill for that purpose might become a law, through the detention of it by the President for ten days. In fact, Mr. Gallatin says that Jefferson, looking to a renewal of the charter, requested him "so to arrange it that it might" thus become a law.

4. Writing to Mr. Jay in 1785, Jefferson advocates a naval force. He says: "I hope our land office will rid us of our debts, and that our first attention then will be to the beginning of a naval force. This alone can countenance our people as carriers on the water, and I suppose them to be determined to continue such." He also advocates a naval armament, for the punishment of outrages upon our citizens, when abroad. Early in 1797, he wrote Mr. Gerry a letter embodying his political creed. In this, he declares himself in favor of "such a naval force only as may protect our coasts and harbors from such depredations as we have experienced," and not of a "navy which, by its own expenses and the eternal wars in which it will implicate us, will grind us with public burdens and sink us under them."

5. In 1790, he assured Mr. Morris that "our prospect (financial) is really a bright one." On December 3d, 1790, he informed M. DeMoustier that "our experiment is going on happily, and that *we need no changes.*" On May 13th, 1791, he communicated to a friend in Europe this gratifying intelligence: "In general, our affairs are proceeding in

a train of unparalleled prosperity, . . . so that I believe I may say with truth, that *there is not a nation under the sun enjoying more present prosperity, nor with more in prospect.*" These three letters, from which the above extracts are taken, were written after the adoption of what Jefferson calls "Hamilton's financial system." Upon turning to the *Ana* we find the following: "Hamilton's financial system had two objects: 1st, as a puzzle, to exclude popular understanding and inquiry; 2d, as a machine for the corruption of the legislature." Jefferson concludes the entry by leaving on record for future generations the monstrous statement, scandalous to the writer, to the government, and to the nation, that the system made the Secretary of the Treasury "*master of every vote in the legislature,* which might give to the government the direction suited to his political views."

6. Jefferson favored the funding of the public debt "as a measure of necessity," and afterwards denounced it.

7. He approved Adams' Defense of the American Constitutions, and subsequently condemned it.

8. He approved the Excise Law, in a letter to Mr Morris, written in 1790, and a few years after, denounced it as unconstitutional, and pronounced it "an infernal law." (Letter to Madison in 1794.)

9. On May 7th, 1783, he believes "that which proposed the conversion of State into Federal debts is one *palatable* ingredient in the pill we are to swallow." And after the United States had assumed the State debts, he writes: "I believe that it—assumption—is harped upon by many, to mark their disaffection to the Government on other grounds." But, in the prefix to his *Ana,* he states that assumption provided "a pabulum for the stock-jobbing herd" of Hamilton.

10. In 1787, he thinks newspapers without a government are preferable to a government without newspapers, and while in the Cabinet, he wrote in his *Ana* that *one newspaper* had saved the Constitution.

In a letter to Mr. Gerry, dated March 29th, 1801, he expresses another opinion of them, as follows : " If they (the public papers) could have continued to get all the loaves and fishes, that is, if I would have gone over to them, they would continue to eulogize. But I well knew that the moment that such removals should take place, as the justice of the preceding administration ought to have executed, their hue and cry would be set up and they would take their old stand. . . . A coalition of sentiments is not for the interest of the printers. They, like the clergy, live by the zeal they can kindle and the schisms they can create." January 2d, 1814, he thus expresses himself: " I deplore with you the *putrid state into which our newspapers have passed*, and the malignity, the vulgarity, and mendacious spirit of those who write for them. These *ordures* are rapidly depraving the public taste and lessening its relish for sound food. As vehicles of information, and a curb to our functionaries, they have rendered themselves useless by forfeiting all title to belief." (Letter to Dr. Walter Jones.)

11. He regretted that the Constitution permitted the re-election of the President, and hoped it would be altered in this respect, yet *was twice elected himself*, favored and promoted the second election of Madison and of Monroe, and suggested a second election to Adams.

12. In February, 1787, he advised Lafayette to use all his efforts to have the new French Constitution assimilated to that of Great Britain as nearly as possible. To John Adams, he wrote that the " English Constitution is acknowledged to be better than all which have preceded it." Yet,

in a certain famous letter he mentioned England as a "*harlot;*" he elsewhere characterized her government as "*the most unprincipled at this day known;*" he spoke in the harshest terms of those who favored a monarchy— styled them "Anglo-men," "Monocrats," and frequently deplored as a great calamity, the very thought of which "oppressed" him, any tendency of this country towards that form of government which he warmly recommended to Lafayette.

13. *Slavery.*—In 1779, Jefferson, as a member of the committee appointed to codify the laws of Virginia, advised the emancipation of all slaves, born in the State after the passage of the act which he drew up, and their colonization at a proper age.

In 1781, he prepared the *Notes on Virginia,* in which he clearly and powerfully set forth the evils of slavery, both to master and slave. "The whole commerce," he writes, "between master and slave is a perpetual exercise of the most boisterous passions, the most unremitting despotism on the one part, and degrading submission on the other." This extract will show the spirit in which he treated the subject. Passing to a consideration of the consequences of slavery, he indulges in the most gloomy forebodings. "*I tremble,*" he exclaims, "*for my country, when I reflect that God is just,* that his justice will not sleep forever, that considering numbers, nature, and natural means only, a revolution of the wheel of fortune . . . is among possible events,—that it may come by supernatural influence. The Almighty has no attribute which can take sides with us in such a contest." The writer further declares that he cannot discuss the matter with composure.

On March 1st, 1784, Jefferson proposed and supported in Congress an ordinance excluding slavery from all the national territory, lying beyond the limits of the States. At that time, according to the opinion of Mr. Madison, Congress had no power over the subject. In 1785, he refused to grant General Chastellenx permission to publish his *Notes on Virginia*, unless the chapters of the book pertaining to slavery in that State *were omitted*. When the Eastern States and Pennsylvania were preparing and passing acts for the liberation of the slaves within their borders, Jefferson wrote private letters respecting "emancipation and expatriation," but made no attempt to set on foot in Virginia a movement to accomplish the one or the other. Alarmed by the massacre of the whites in Santo Domingo, he cried out: "If something is not done (with slavery) we shall be the *murderers of our children*." Notwithstanding this alarming apprehension, he still held his slaves, and did nothing. Dreading that slavery might bring about the slaughter of his own and his friends' children, he moved not a finger to avert so terrible a calamity. Some time during the year 1814, he wrote to a young Mr. Cole a letter, in which he suggested that young men should not abandon their slave property. Mr. Cole, however, emancipated his negroes, took them to the West, and there provided homes for them. In February, 1817, Jefferson informed Dr. Humphreys that he was "in favor of the gradual retirement (of the negroes), and their establishment elsewhere in freedom." In 1820, and 1821, while the question of admitting Missouri into the Union was pending before Congress, he favored her admission as a slave State, and opposed restrictions on slavery in the territory acquired from France. Extracts from some letters of his, written about this time, will serve to show his opinions on these subjects. In a letter to General Breckenridge in 1821, he objects to the sending of young Southerners to Northern colleges, for fear of their "imbibing opinions and principles in discord with those of *their own country*." A letter, written in the same year to J. C. Cabell, contains the following: " How many of our youths she (Harvard College) now has learning the lessons of anti-Missourianism, I know not. . . . These will return home, no doubt, deeply impressed with the sacred principles of our Holy Alliance of Restrictionists"—of slavery. On August 17th, 1821, he thus writes General Dearborn: " Whether the question (Missouri) is dead or only sleepeth, I know not. I see only that it has given resurrection to the Hartford Convention men. They have had the address, by playing on the honest feelings of our former friends, to seduce them from their former kindred spirits. . . . They have adroitly wriggled into power under the auspices of morality, and now are again in the ascendancy, from which their sins had hurled them." Mr. Jefferson could not believe that Northern men were disinterested in their opposition to slavery.

In his memoir of his own life, composed in 1821, he thus expresses himself: " Nothing is more certainly written in the book of fate, than that these people are to be free; nor is it less certain that the two races, equally free, cannot live in the same government. Nature, habit, and opinion have drawn indelible lines of distinction between them. It is still in our power to direct the process of emancipation and deportation peacefully, and in such slow degree, as that the evil will wear off insensibly. If, on the contrary, it is left to force itself on, human nature must shudder at the prospect held up. We should in vain look for an example in the Spanish deportation or deletion of the Moors. This precedent would fall far short of our case."

Writing to Mr. Short in 1823, he says: " We feel and deplore it (the existence of slavery) morally and politically," etc. Jefferson clearly perceived the evils, moral and political, of slavery, and vividly portrayed them, but did little or nothing to eradicate, or even diminish them. During his lifetime, most of the Northern States provided for the gradual abolition of slavery, and hundreds of southern men manumitted their negroes, but he, *for forty-five years,* kept up that baleful " commerce between master and slave," the ill effects of which he points out in his *Notes on Virginia.* Washington, at his death, set free all his slaves, and enjoined upon his executors, to provide a " regular and permanent fund" for those unable to support themselves. Jefferson wrote fine sounding phrases about the rights of man, the wrong of slavery, and its direful consequences, but, while he lived, never loosed the bonds of a single slave, not even those of Burwell, who saved his life, and was otherwise so faithful. In making his will, too, he forgot this friend. By a codicil to the will, he manumitted Burwell and four others. Mr. Jefferson, no doubt, originally desired the abolition of slavery throughout the country; but the labor of his negroes proved profitable, and in this, as in other matters, his better impulses were checked by his lust for popularity, combined with the obligations of party fealty.

14. On October 8th, 1787, Jefferson wrote of Louis XVI.: "The king goes for nothing. He hunts one-half the day, is drunk the other half, and signs whatever he is bid." On April 6th, 1790, he states that this same king is, " A prince, the model of royal excellence."

15. He *signed the Alien Law, and the Sedition Law as Vice-President,* and, still being Vice-President, prepared the Resolutions of 1798, in which he pronounced those laws not laws, *but absolutely void.*

16. In December, 1787, in a letter to Mr. Madison, Jef-

ferson, the champion of the people, and the advocate of universal equality, expresses a doubt whether the members of the House of Representatives, when elected by the people, would be as well qualified for their duties as they would be, if chosen by the legislatures of the States.

17. This same stickler for popular equality suggested that one house of the Virginia Legislature—he preferred the Senate—should represent the *wealth* of the State.

18. He wished all kings swept from the earth, but thought most of the nations of Europe incapable of self-government.

19. The characteristic vacillation of Jefferson is illustrated by his varying opinions in regard to the Constitution. To one he writes: There are very good articles in it, and very bad." To another: "I confess there are things in it which stagger all my disposition to subscribe to what such an assembly has proposed." In 1787, he thinks, "All the good in this new Constitution might have been couched in three or four new articles, to be added to the good old and venerable fabric, *which should have been preserved*." (Letter to Adams.)

In 1789, writing to Dr. Humphreys, he extols this same new Constitution, as the "*wisest ever presented to man.*" In a letter to A. Donald, he thus discourses respecting it: " I wish with all my soul that the nine first Conventions may accept the Constitution; this will secure to us the good it contains, which, I think, is great and important. But I equally wish that the four latest Conventions, whichever they be, may refuse to execute it, till a Declaration of Rights be annexed." Upon further reflection, he favored the " Massachusetts plan " of adopting first, and amending afterwards.

20. Mr. Jefferson's remaining in the Cabinet, while he opposed many of the prominent measures of Washington's

administration, and even seemed anxious to embarrass it, involves a question not only of consistency, but of self-respect. Alexander Hamilton admirably discusses the duty of a Cabinet officer in this regard, with special reference to Jefferson's conduct, in an open letter signed Metellus, from which we take the following paragraph: " If he can not coalesce with those with whom he is associated, as far as the rules of official decorum, propriety, and obligation may require, without abandoning what he conceives to be the interests of the community, let him not cling to the honor or the emolument of an office, whichever it be, that attracts him. Let him renounce a situation which is a clog upon his patriotism, and tell the people he could no longer continue in it without forfeiting his duty to them; that he has quitted it to serve them. Such is the course that would be pursued by a man attentive to unite the sense of delicacy with the sense of duty—in earnest about the pernicious tendency of public measures, and more solicitous to act the disinterested friend of the people, than the interested, ambitious, and intriguing head of a party." Mr. Jefferson, while Secretary of State, indirectly encouraged, if he did not directly instigate, attacks upon Washington and upon his administration. Hamilton, in a letter signed "An American," having asked whether it was possible that the head of the principal department of the government could be " the patron of a paper, the evident object of which was to decry the government and its measures," thus proceeds: " If he disapproves of the government itself, and thinks it deserving of his opposition, can he reconcile it to his own personal dignity and the principles of probity, to hold an office under it, and employ *the means of official influence* in that opposition? If he disapproves of the leading measures adopted in the course of his (?) administration, can he reconcile it with the principles of propriety and delicacy to hold a place in that administration, and at the same time, be instrumental in vilifying measures, which have been adopted by both branches of the Legislature, and sanctioned by the Chief Magistrate of the United States." These papers, signed respectively "An American" and "Metellus," should be read by every one desirous of forming a correct estimate of Jefferson and Hamilton. No reply to either of them was made by Jefferson.

21. Just before signing, as Secretary of State, Washington's proclamation against the Western rioters, Jefferson complained to Madison of being "forced to appear to approve what I have condemned uniformly." It is difficult to understand the mental and moral nature of a person who, in view of the facts, could write these words. One can scarcely imagine how a brave and honorable man, in performing the duties of a Cabinet officer, can be forced to seem to approve what he condemns.

CHAPTER VIII.

JEFFERSON'S APPREHENSIONS OF MONARCHY.

Jefferson seems to have been haunted by the perpetual fear of our return to monarchy, and to have believed that there really was in the country an organized party, striving to accomplish that result. He falls into despondency, in contemplation of so dire a calamity; he burns with indignation against those who would bring it upon the people; is "almost oppressed with the apprehension that we shall be driven back to the land, from which we launched, twenty years ago." He brands fabulous friends of monarchial institutions as "Monocrats;" like a political Don Quixote, he assails imaginary "apostates" from republican principles, with the Mazzei letter; he raves about the "*energumenoi* of royalty," till one is tempted to believe that he himself is a demoniac. The two persons, whom Jefferson thought most grievously afflicted with this monarchial mania, were John Adams, and Alexander Hamilton. These were the leading and most influential plotters against the liberties of the people. Washington was their dupe and instrument—the lay figure upon which the chief conspirators hung "the rags of royalty," with which Jefferson declared he was enveloped. But the arch-fiend, the Lucifer of the revolt against free government, was Hamilton. What were the reasons for all this solicitude and indignation? There were none. The only pretext for them was that Washington, Adams, Marshall, Jay, Hamilton and other men of wisdom believed that the Federal government should possess more power than Jefferson thought it ought to have. From this difference of opinion, Jefferson inferred their desire for the restoration of monarchy. When he mentioned his fears of royalty to Washington, the General ridiculed the idea, and said that in his opinion there "were not ten men in the United States, who entertained such a thought." On another occasion Washington, incensed at the press insinuations that he, favored a monarchy, vehemently declared that he regretted having accepted the presidency a second time—that he would rather be on his farm than to be made emperor of the world, and yet they were charging him with wanting to be a king. (The *Ana*, August 2d, 1793). Jefferson, in a letter to Mr. Van Buren, admits that Hamilton said the idea of a monarchy was visionary, and in a conversation with the same gentleman, expressed his belief in Hamilton's "frankness in regard to public matters." In a private letter written in May, 1792, to his friend Colonel Carrington, to whom he would most certainly state his real opinions, Hamilton says "I am firmly attached to the republican theory," and stigmatized "any attempt to subvert the system of the country, as both criminal and visionary." That Hamilton was not amenable to the charge of endeavoring to overthrow our form of government, seems clear enough. Jefferson's theory of a royalist party was dealt a most damaging blow by John Adams. On July 17th, 1791, he wrote to the Massachusetts statesman a letter, in which he remarked that their difference as to the best form of government was well known to both of them; Adams, on July 29th, replied that he had never had a serious conversation with Jefferson on the subject, and that any allusions to it or mention of it between them had always been made in a jocular or imperfect manner. "If you suppose," he continues, "that I ever had a design or a desire of attempting to introduce a government of Kings, Lords and Commons; or in other words, an hereditary executive or an hereditary senate either into the government of the United States, or of any individual state, you are wholly mistaken. . . . . I beg you, if you have ever put such a construction upon anything said by me, that you will mention it, and I will undertake to convince you that it has no such meaning." To this direct denial and call for evidence there was no reply. It thus appears, that the three persons whom Jefferson most strongly charged with endeavoring to subvert the republic, disavowed any design or desire to restore a monarchy. Their reputation should render their disavowal conclusive. But the theory that these men or their associates purposed a return to monarchial institutions, is inherently most improbable; men, by whose efforts and abilities the colonies had been transformed into independent states, and provided with a certain form of free government, would hardly be so unstable as to attempt or wish a change of that form, before its efficiency had been fully tested. Had there been any who desired to re-establish royalty, they must have had little discernment indeed, not to perceive that the popular love of freedom, and hatred of regal power, would render abortive all schemes for effecting such re-establishment. No proofs of the existence of a monarchial party were offered. When Adams called upon Jefferson for evidence that the former favored the introduction of hereditary institutions, the latter, as above stated, was silent. In a letter to Washington, dated August 18th, 1792, Hamilton replies to the allegation that there is a royalist party in the country, in this effective manner; " to this there is no other answer than a flat denial, except this; that the project from its absurdity defeats itself. The idea of introducing a monarchy or an aristocracy into this country, by employing the influence of a government continually changing hands, towards it, is one of those visionary things that none but madmen could meditate, and that *no wise man will believe.* If it could be done at all, which is utterly incredible, it would require a long series of time, certainly beyond the life of any individual, to effect it. Who then would enter into such a plot? To hope that the people may be cajoled into giving their sanction to such institutions, is still more chimerical. A people so enlightened and so diversified as the people of this country, can surely never be brought to it, but from convulsions and disorders in consequence of threats of popular demagogues. The truth unquestionably, is that the only path to the subversion of the republican system of the country is, by flattering the prejudices of the people, and exciting their jealousies and apprehensions, to throw affairs into confusion and bring on civil war. Tired at length of anarchy, they may take shelter in the arms of monarchy for repose and security. . . . . . .

Those, then, who resist a confirmation of public order are the true artificers of monarchy." These are the words of a statesman, and, therefore, they are quite different from those of self-seeking demagogues. In the letter to Washington, containing the allegation that Hamilton answers as above, Jefferson states that the same parties who then desired a monarchy, endeavored to establish one in the Constitutional Convention. Hamilton shows that but few of those who sat in the Convention were, at the time Jefferson wrote, potential in public affairs, and declares that in that body every one agreed that the British form of government, though possessing much merit, was out of the question in this country. As he had been a member of the Convention, and Jefferson during its session was in Europe, it is easy to determine whose statement is the more likely to be correct. Moreover, Mr. Madison, also a member, substantially sustains Hamilton in regard to the sentiments of the Convention.

There is little doubt that Jefferson's apprehensions of a return to monarchy were groundless. Some believe that they were entirely feigned.

CHAPTER IX.

JEFFERSON AND THE DECLARATION OF INDEPENDENCE.

Mr. Jefferson's admirers are never weary of extolling him for composing the Declaration of Independence. The inscription on his tomb, prepared by himself, informs all the world that he regarded that document as one of the three great works of his life, one of his title deeds to fame. A little attention to the history of the paper, and to its contents, may dissipate some of the prevalent illusions respecting its authorship, and its intrinsic merits.

The Declaration, with which we are familiar, whatever its merits or defects, is by no means the same that was drafted by Jefferson. Of the Declaration prepared by him, Congress struck out more than one-fourth, and made numerous amendments of the remainder. It is very probable that much more would have been discarded, but for the efforts of John Adams, who possessed great influence in the Congress, and who, having conceived a high regard for the author, generously and vigorously defended the document. Jefferson, long afterwards, described Adams's arguments in its behalf as, in the highest degree, powerful and convincing, characterizing him as a very Colossus in the protracted debate. The Declaration contains little that was new, except the arrangement. The grievances enumerated in it had been repeatedly set forth. It is compiled, with some change of language, mainly from four documents, issued by the first Continental Congress in 1774, to wit: A Declaration of Rights; An Address to the People of Great Britain;

A Memorial to the Inhabitants of the Colonies; and A Petition to the King of Great Britain. Its opening somewhat resembles the beginning of the Memorial just mentioned, "separation" being substituted for "opposition." The short, paragraphic style, so effective in it, is borrowed from the Petition to the King. Some of the most telling passages are taken from the Mecklenburg Declaration of Independence, adopted May 20th, 1775.

A few examples of the amendments made will show how much they were needed. "Inherent and inalienable rights," found in the original, was changed to "certain inalienable rights." In the clause, "to expunge their former systems of government," "alter" is substituted for "expunge." "A history of unremitting injuries" was amended by putting "repeated" in the place of "unremitting." The passage, "He has suffered the administration of justice totally to cease in some of these States, refusing his assent to laws," was remodelled so as to read, "He has obstructed the administration of justice by refusing his assent to laws." From the sentence, "He has kept among us in times of peace standing armies and ships of war," the last four words were omitted, there being, perhaps, some doubts as to the ability even of a king to keep among us ships of war. In the original was the following: "To prove this, let facts be submitted to a candid world, for the truth of which we pledge a faith yet unsullied by falsehood." From this sentence was stricken the clause after "world." The original draft contained such verbiage as this: "Future ages will scarcely believe that the hardiness of one man adventured, within the short compass of twelve years only, to lay a foundation so broad, and so undisguised for tyranny over a people fostered and fixed in principles of freedom;" and such fustian as this: "We (British and Americans) might have been a free and a great people together, but a communication of grandeur and of freedom, it seems, is below their dignity. Be it so, since they will have it. The road to happiness and to glory is open to us too." The following reads like the production of a sentimental young woman: "These facts have given the last stab to agonizing affection, and manly spirit bids us to renounce forever these unfeeling brethren. We must endeavor to forget our former love for them."

Some of the grievances complained of did not exist. For example, Parliament had passed no law depriving the colonists of trial by jury. The Declaration asserts that the king "has plundered our seas, ravaged our coasts, burnt our towns." It would have been difficult for its author to verify this terrible and preposterous accusation against his majesty. Throughout the document, the Colonies are improperly styled States. This error was, in several places, corrected by the Congress. The parts taken from the Mecklenburg Declaration are the reference to inherent rights, the clause declaring that the Colonies "are and of right ought to be" independent States, those clauses pronouncing their absolution from allegiance to the British crown, and the dissolution of all political connection with Great Britain, and the concluding pledge of lives, fortunes, and sacred honors. In borrowing from the Mecklenburg paper, the word "inalienable" before "rights" was substituted for "undeniable." The latter is certainly the proper word. There are no such things as inalienable rights. A free man can alienate some of his rights, or all of them. He, who is incapable of doing this, is not a free man.

In the Declaration as it now stands, the last paragraph is the best. It is characterized by a clear, strong, and animated diction, that stirs the blood, and has won for it deserved admiration. The draft of the paragraph, as reported by the committee, is as follows: "We, therefore, the Representatives of the United States of America in General Congress assembled, do, in the name and by the authority of the good people of these States, reject and renounce all allegiance and subjection to the kings of Great Britain, and all others who may hereafter claim by, through, or under them; we utterly dissolve all political connection which may heretofore have subsisted between us and the people or Parliament of Great Britain; and finally, we do assert and declare these Colonies to be free and independent States; and that as free and independent States they have full power to levy war, conclude peace, contract alliances, establish commerce, and to do all other acts and things which independent States may of right do. And for the support of this declaration, we mutually pledge to each other our lives, our fortunes, and our sacred honor." As has been stated, the final sentence, the most telling part of this paragraph, is borrowed from another paper.

The inferiority of the original paragraph to the amended one, is manifest. It will be seen that in the former, there is no invocation of Divine Providence, nor is there such invocation anywhere in the Declaration prepared by the committee. The absence of this is one of its chief defects. The Declaration, although expurgated and amended by the Congress, is exaggerated in statement, turgid and redundant in style, and needlessly long. An examination of the first paragraph, the exclusive work of Mr. Jefferson, reveals the serious defects concealed beneath its flowing language. The clause immediately following the opening "when," is superfluous, since, the necessity of dissolving the bands mentioned, must come if it come at all, in the course of human events. The paragraph intimates, that the ordinary course of affairs brings about the necessity of dissolution, that the advent of such necessity is of frequent occurrence, whereas, in reality, the necessity for separation rarely if ever arises, though the separation may often be desirable or advantageous. It is assumed, that one of the peoples has not only the sole right, but the ability to effect the dissolution, although both of them are alike interested in the matter, and the one attempting a forcible separation may, and often does fail. The colonists and the British are treated as two peoples, while in fact, they were then the same people, in the sense of the word as there employed.

Not only does it become necessary for some citizens of a nation, who are styled a people, to effect the dissolution aforesaid, whether they can or can not, but it becomes necessary for them to assume a separate and equal station among the powers of the earth. The separation, if accomplished, would probably give them a separate station, but how shall a feeble people take an equal station among the strong powers of the earth? Why such a question? The station to be assumed, is that " equal station, (equal to what?) to which " certain laws entitle the people. Surely, this is clear enough. These laws are of two kinds, the laws of nature, and the laws of nature's God. Many persons believe that the laws of nature, and those of nature's God are the same, but one author seems to have had a different opinion.

In the paragraph, the residents of the Colonies are referred to as "one people." This term may mean a race, as for instance, the Jewish people. Its other meaning is an organized political society, a nation. It is evident that the author employs it in the latter sense, for he sets it in opposition to Great Britain, confessedly a nation. A nation possesses independence and sovereignty. Were the Colonies when they declared their independence, already independent? They were not so then, and never had been. Their inhabitants were at the time, citizens of Great Britain, subjects of the British king, to whom they had repeatedly acknowledged their allegiance. The very paper in which the term is found clearly establishes these facts. A war of seven years was required to secure for them independence and sovereignty, the essential attributes of a nation. What, then, could be more erroneous than to style them a "people?"

The cause assigned for drawing up the Declaration is worthy of notice. There were excellent reasons for preparing and publishing such a paper. It would present in one group, and in a formal manner, the wrongs inflicted upon the Colonies by the Crown, and the grievances of which they complained, so that the people might clearly comprehend the motives which urged the Congress to adopt the momentous resolution of severing their connection with the mother country, and thereby be induced to sustain the movement. It would tend to produce unity of thought, feeling of action. It would inspirit the army, confirm the wavering, encourage the timid, arouse the indifferent. It might enable the Congress to borrow money, or negotiate treaties, which could not be done without such declaration. It might bring to the Colonies, in the impending contest, the assistance of some nation, or monarch hostile to England. These, and similar reasons would seem to be sufficient to account for the preparation of the Document. But it appears from the paragraph, that members of the Congress were not moved in this matter by any such considerations. They were prompted by "a decent respect for the opinions of mankind." Is it possible that the immortal Declaration was drafted, discussed, adopted and published for that reason only? Did John Adams for three days, defend it against the assaults of its enemies, out of regard for the opinions of mankind? Or did Mr. Jefferson merely ascribe to others the feeling which impelled him to favor it? This clause, and his desire to submit "facts to a candid world," remind one of an incident in the life of Anacharsis Clootz, a notorious atheist of the French Revolution. Clootz, though a German, sat in the National Convention. When some one demanded of him, by what right, he a German, occupied a seat in the National Convention of France, he replied that he was a *Representative of the human race*. Since atheists believe there is no Supreme Ruler of the Universe, they can appeal to nothing wiser or higher than the human race. It is probable that Jefferson, while resident in France, acquired from them the habit, observable in his writing, of invoking the judgment, or approval of mankind.

The second paragraph is also the work of Jefferson. It opens with the statement of several propositions, that are declared to be self-evident truths. It is doubtful, whether a single one of them embodies a self-evident truth. Two of them are manifestly untrue, to wit: the proposition "that all men are created equal," and the proposition "that they are endowed by their Creator with certain inalienable rights." Who does not know that at birth, which may be said to mark the end of creation, men are unequal, socially, physically and mentally? They differ in health, some inheriting disease, and others being corporally sound; in strength, in size, in rank, in possessions. They are even morally unlike, some being tainted with a hereditary tendency to vice or crime, for the iniquity of fathers is visited upon their children. Nor do men, at birth, possess equal rights. Such may have been originally the case, under the law of nature, but that law has been so modified, in its operation, by municipal and other laws, resulting from the necessities of society, that the rights of men, in one nation, differ from those rights, in another nation, and, even in the same country, some persons have certain rights that others do not possess. The doctrine of "inalienable" rights has been elsewhere shown to be untenable.

Mr. Jefferson seems unfortunate here in his choice of language respecting human rights. He declares that men are endowed by their Creator with certain rights; he names as one of those rights, the pursuit of happiness. The logical deduction is that the Creator has endowed men with the pursuit of happiness, which is an absurdity. He no doubt meant to say "Among these" are the right to life, the right to liberty, and the right to the pursuit of happiness. That men have an indefeasible natural right to life, and to liberty, is indisputable, but the proposition that they have such a right to pursue their own happiness, must be accepted with some qualification. All the remaining propositions, here enunciated, have been, or can be denied or questioned by thoughtful men, and cannot, therefore, be regarded as self-evident truths.

Further on, the author, if his own words be taken in their ordinary signification, intimates that some unnamed person, who governs the whole earth, harbors the design of reducing mankind "under an absolute despotism," and assures his fellow creatures that it is their right and their duty to throw off the government of this universal tyrant. What a spectacle would be presented by the human race struggling to resist an impending despotism! The attention of the reader is next arrested by this remarkable period, which we present in the form that it bore, before amendment:
"The history of the present king of Great Britain is a

history of unremitting injuries and usurpations, among which appears no solitary fact to contradict the uniform tenor of the rest, but all have in direct object, the establishment of an absolute tyranny over these states." Here are two very awkwardly expressed allegations; first, that the king, since his accession, has been continually engaged in the work of injury and usurpation; second, that the sole purpose of this unremitting work has been, and is to establish a tyranny over his American Colonies. In other words, the monarch of a powerful and populous kingdom has, for sixteen years, been devoting his time and attention exclusively to the task of imposing a tyranny upon some thousands of his loyal subjects, dwelling in another hemisphere.

The paragraph closes with the rash offer to prove this extravagant statement, to *the world*. It is fair to say that the first and second paragraphs are more objectionable than the others. Indeed, the document as a whole is by no means devoid of merit. The arrangement is proper, the language generally good, the style flowing, sometimes strong, occasionally elevated. The wrongs inflicted upon our fathers by the British Government are vigorously set forth. But while it is admitted that our valued Declaration possesses merit, it is not admitted that Jefferson deserves the high praise accorded to him as its author. On the contrary, it seems clear from the following considerations, that he does not deserve it: 1. He did not suggest the preparation of such a paper. 2. He did little to secure its adoption. 3. He is not the sole author of it. It is true that most of it is his work; but the Congress, by omitting a great deal of his original draft, and making many alterations in the remainder, did much to impart to it its present popular form. 4. The omissions and alterations greatly improved the original. 5. The Declaration, though bettered by expurgation and amendments, is yet far from being a masterpiece. We have seen how obnoxious to criticism some portions of it are. 6. The renown which the written Declaration has brought Jefferson is partly attributable to the grandeur of the deed with which it is associated. The act of declaring the Colonies free and independent was an act of such transcendent importance in our history, that it rendered famous even the man, who prepared the form of words in which it was done. The paper styled the Declaration of Independence is not venerated by us on account of its excellence as a piece of composition, but because it is the new *Magna Charta* of our ancestral liberties; because it explains and vindicates a transaction which marked the dawn of a better, a glorious era, a transaction, without which, the independence, the prosperity, and the power of these United States would have been impossible; because it reminds us that our fathers belonged to a race accustomed to the rights of freemen; that they regarded them as of inestimable value, and that they were willing to risk life and fortune in order to transmit those rights, as a precious heritage, to their children. 7. For more than a quarter of a century, Jefferson was the idol of a majority of the American people. The multitude, even more than the individual, is disposed to overlook the faults, and magnify the merits of its favorite. The Declaration is the best of his literary works, of which there are few; it treats, too, of something in which every man is profoundly interested. It is not at all surprising, then, that the people deemed it a production of extraordinary excellence. Demagogues, courting the favor of the democratic elements in society, found it profitable to praise Jefferson and his works, and, of course, lauded the Declaration to the skies, thus perpetuating and strengthening the erroneous opinion of its merits, originally formed. This was the more easily done, because all were inclined to view with favor whatever was written by one who had assisted to lay the foundations of the republic. To the popular affection for Jefferson, and to the laudation of him by demagogues, some of them gifted with great ability, is to be ascribed, we believe, much of the honor that has been accorded to him, as author of the Declaration of Independence.

CHAPTER X.

SOME REMARKABLE POLITICAL THEORIES.

1. Jefferson proposed a Commission, to consist of one Congressional representative from each State, which should have the same powers as Congress, and sit permanently, while Congress was not in session. One such Commission was appointed, but it soon became the scene of such bitter disputation, as to render further consultation on public measures impossible. In a short time, it ceased to assemble, its powers expired, and no other was ever appointed.—Morse's *Life of Hamilton*.

2. In 1787, after an experience of seven years had conclusively shown that the Articles of Confederation were totally inadequate to the indispensable purposes of a national government, after every State had recognized this inadequacy by appointing delegates to a Convention for organizing a new Constitution, and when the Convention was actually in session, Jefferson still believed that the Government of the Confederation, was "without comparison the best existing, or that ever did exist."—*Letter to Mr. Carrington*.

3. In the same letter, he expresses these opinions: that Congress had power under the Confederation to enforce contributions of money from the several States; that "it was not necessary to give Congress that power expressly; they have it by the law of nature," and that "compulsion was never so easy as in our (?) this, case." It is well known that no State admitted the possession by Congress of the power

mentioned, and that Congress did not claim such power, or attempt to exercise it. As early as July, 1782, the Legislature of New York unanimously resolved, "That experience has demonstrated the Confederation to be defective in several essential points, particularly in not vesting the Federal Government with the power of providing revenue for itself." In April, 1783, the Congress of the Confederation passed resolutions recommending to the several States to invest the Congress with certain specified powers for raising revenue, to restore and maintain the public credit. In February, 1786, a committee, consisting of Messrs. King, Pinckney, Kean, Monroe, and Petit in their report to Congress, say, that "It most clearly appeared, that the requisitions of Congress for eight years, have been so irregular in their operation, so uncertain in their collection, and so evidently unproductive, that a reliance on them in future, as a source from whence moneys are to be drawn to discharge the engagements of the Confederacy, . . . would be not less *dishonorable to the understandings* of those who entertain such confidence; that it would be dangerous to the welfare and peace of the Union," and recommend that Congress should represent to the several States "the utter impossibility of maintaining and preserving the faith of the Federal government, by temporary requisitions on the States." The Congress agreed to this report. What Congress deemed it utterly impossible to do, Jefferson declared could be most easily performed. His opinion that Congress possessed the power under consideration, is hardly so remarkable as his declaration that the power results from the Law of Nature. It is scarcely possible that any citizen of the United States, except Mr. Jefferson, could deduce such a power from that law. But how does he propose to enforce the power. "A single frigate would soon levy on the commerce of any state the deficiency of its contributions." Nothing could be more simple, or more summary. Yet the founders of the Republic, strangely enough, bore their financial troubles for eight years, without resorting to this efficacious method of terminating them. Congress again and again, appealed to the States, and to their citizens to discharge their requisitions. They were reminded of their "plighted faith;"—that the public debt had been contracted for the common benefit. They were assured that "justice, honor, and gratitude" demanded the payment of their quotas. They were warned that the cause of liberty, which they had engaged to vindicate, would be "blotted" by the failure of the Confederation to fulfil its engagements. Appeals, reminders, and warnings were attended with but partial success, but the Representatives in Congress, dullards that they were, never tried the effect of a "single frigate," operating against the commerce of a State. Had they done this, all would have been well.

4. He entertained curious notions respecting the re-eligibility of the president, allowed by the Constitution. He wrote the " President will be a bad edition of a Polish king. He may be elected from four years to four years, for life. Reason and experience prove to us that a chief magistrate so continuable, is an office for life. When one or two generations shall have proved that there is an office for life, it becomes, on every succession, worthy of intrigue, of bribery, force and even of foreign interference. It will be of great consequence to France and England, to have America governed by a Gallo-man, or an Anglo-man. Once in office, and possessing the military force of the Union, without the aid or check of a council, he would not be easily dethroned, even if the people could be induced to withdraw their votes from him." This quotation from a

letter, written to John Adams in November, 1787, shows what vagaries may emanate from the brain of a sage. It is apparent, that in regard to the matter under consideration, he possessed little of the experience, and less of the reason to which he appeals in support of his views. Again, alluding to the subject in a letter to Mr. Madison, dated December 20th, 1787, he states his fear that in cases of close elections, the President " will pretend false votes, foul play, and hold possession of the reins of government," and that, if the people were disposed to vote him out, foreign powers would not permit it, if his continuance in office would promote their interests.

5. He styled the people of the United States under the Constitution, "a Society," and, oddly enough, called the suppression of the Whiskey Rebellion, " arming one portion of the society against another."

6. He designated Virginia as his "country," and the United States courts as " foreign jurisdictions," although he *was at the time Vice-President of the United States, as well as a citizen of Virginia.*

7. In 1797, Jefferson wrote to Mr. Monroe a letter, in which he recommended that some means be devised to punish residents of Virginia for attempting to transfer to the Federal courts, suits brought by or against them in the tribunals of that State. In the year named, Justice Iredell of the United States Supreme Court, delivered a charge to the grand jury, in the United States court at Richmond, whereupon the jury presented certain circular letters of several members of Congress, among them, that of Samuel J. Cabell, of Virginia. Jefferson desired to punish, through the courts of the State, those by whose agency the presentments were made. Hence his letter to Monroe. He proposed that the Legislature should enact a law, declaring

that a " plea to the jurisdiction of a State court, or the reclamation of a foreign jurisdiction, if adjudged valid, would be safe, but if adjudged invalid, should be followed by the punishment of *præmunire* for the attempt." The crime of *præmunire*, under the English law, was a contempt of the king's authority, manifested by the introduction, or the attempt to introduce, a foreign authority into the realm. The law of *præmunire* was enacted to check Papal aggressions in Great Britain, and the punishment of one convicted of invoking the Pope's protection was banishment, the forfeiture of lands and goods, loss of member, or, of life itself. In order to protect State rights, not from actual, but from apprehended invasion, Mr. Jefferson would attack the great common-law right of every freeman, to question the authority of the tribunal, that assumes to try him or his cause. He proposed to assail this precious right by passing an unconstitutional law, for under the Federal Constitution the citizen has, in many cases, the privilege of removing his cause from a State to a Federal court. It is true, the proposed law did not forbid him to apply for a removal; it only punished him in case his application was unsuccessful. But how many would make the application, at the risk of being subjected to the pains and penalties of *præmunire?* It was a tyrannical law. It admitted the existence of a right, but sought to deprive the citizen of it by means at once indirect and cruel. By the enactment of such a law, the Legislature of Virginia would virtually say to every one within her borders: You have, indeed, the right to be tried by a Federal court, when charged with a certain offence; nevertheless, in such case, we will bring you before one of our State courts, and if you there ask for your acknowledged rights and are refused, or if you even presume to plead to the jurisdiction of the State tribunal, and your plea is not sustained, you will be punished with fine, banishment, or death. Such a law would be a blot on the statute book of an enlightened State, and is fit only for the code of a Draco.

It is superfluous to say that neither the law suggested by Jefferson—a law begotten by spite, and born of folly—nor any similar law, was ever enacted in Virginia.

8. In the year 1798, Mr. Jefferson drafted nine resolutions, a copy of which he sent to George Nicholas, of Kentucky. His purpose was to have them adopted by the Legislature of that State, and the Legislatures of other States. These resolutions, modified, have become famous, under the name of "the Kentucky Resolutions of '98," frequently contracted to "the Resolutions of '98."

The *first* affirmed that the Federal Constitution is a compact between the States, to which each of the thirteen States is a party; that "each party has an equal right to judge for itself, as well of infractions of the compact, as of the mode and measure of redress."

The *second* declares that the Constitution has delegated to Congress a power to punish treason, counterfeiting the securities and current coin of the United States, piracies and felonies committed on the high seas, and offences against the law of nations, and "no other crimes whatsoever." There is not a native-born man in the country, who does not know that Congress has power to punish other offences, for example, offences pertaining to the mails.

The *fifth* applies the right alleged in the first, to three Acts of the preceding Congress: the Alien Law, the Sedition Law, and the Law to punish counterfeiting the notes of the United States Bank, each of which three laws is pronounced in the resolution, "*not law, but altogether void and of no force.*"

The *seventh* postpones action upon sundry other Congressional enactments, until they can be subjected to "revisal and correction."

The *eighth* directs the appointment of a "Committee of Conference and Correspondence," who are to communicate the foregoing resolutions to the several States, and inform them that Kentucky, with all her esteem for the co-States and for the Union, is determined "to submit to undelegated, and, consequently, unlimited powers in no man or body of men on earth," and "that any State has a natural right, in cases not within the compact, to *nullify*, of its own authority, all assumptions of power by others within its limits."

It further authorizes and instructs the Committee aforesaid, to ask the co-States "to concur in declaring these acts void and of no force, and each to take measures of its own for providing that neither of these acts, nor any other of the General Government, not plainly and intentionally authorized by the Constitution, shall be exercised within their respective limits." In this resolution, too, it is set forth that any appeal or communication to Congress in regard to acts deemed unconstitutional is manifestly improper, since Congress is no party to the compact, but merely its creature."

The *ninth* gives to the said Committee power to correspond with other like committees, to be appointed by the "co-States," and requires a report of its proceedings to be made to the next session of the Legislature.

Mr. Nicholas was wise enough not to submit all of these resolutions to the Legislature of Kentucky. He rejected the eighth and ninth, and substituted for them two drawn up by himself, the purport of which was, that the seven preceding resolutions should be laid before Congress by the Senators and Representatives of Kentucky; that they should use their best endeavors to procure the repeal of the obnoxious acts at the next session, and should ask the Representatives of the other States to concur with them in the effort to effect this repeal. Not a single State Legislature adopted the resolutions, so carefully elaborated by Jefferson. That of Kentucky passed seven of them, together with Mr. Nicholas's substitutes for the eighth and ninth. The Virginia Legislature adopted resolutions similar in spirit to those of Jefferson, and less objectionable in language, but omitted entirely the clause which declared void the three laws specified by him. The resolutions of Kentucky were never laid before Congress. The Legislatures of *ten* States disavowed the right of a State Legislature to decide on the validity of Acts of Congress.

Had the resolutions of Jefferson been adopted and acted upon by the several States, or by two or three of the strong ones, at or about the time they were drafted, it is clear that there would have been a collision between the Federal Government and some of the States; the recalcitrant States would have withdrawn from the Union, for the central authority was not then powerful enough to prevent this, even had it made the attempt, and the child of the Revolution, now a mighty nation, would have died in its cradle.

Scattered broadcast by the party successors of Jefferson, these resolutions, like the dragon's teeth sown by Cadmus, sprang up armed men, armed for the destruction of the Republic. They embody a great political heresy, the doctrine of state-sovereignty—not of state-rights—but of *state-sovereignty*, a distinction of incalculable importance. This heretical monster *slew five hundred thousand* of those people whom Jefferson professed to love so well, cost the nation *three billions of treasure*, burdened her with an enormous debt, beneath which she now groans, and suddenly set loose in our midst millions of ignorant, degraded beings, to disseminate among us vice, superstition, disease and crime. This monster's existence was incompatible with the existence of the nation, and he was doomed to death. He was executed by the flaming sword of war, perished amid the thunders of battle, perished beyond the hope of resurrection. *Sic semper hostibus patriæ!* Long live the Republic!

9. Mr. Jefferson thought it desirable that the Supreme Court should possess a veto power, similar to that of the President.

10. He held that it was better for the welfare of the people to have newspapers without a government, than a government without newspapers. It seems incredible that a sane man could enunciate such a proposition, but in a letter, dated January 16th, 1787, written by him from Paris to Edward Carrington, are these words: "Were it left to me to decide whether we should have a government without newspapers, or newspapers without a government, *I should not hesitate a moment to prefer the latter.*"

11. Jefferson approved and defended the Democratic clubs of his day. These clubs were not the harmless associations which in our time bear the same name. Washington, in a letter to Burgess Ball, writes: "The Democratic Society of Philadelphia, from which the others have emanated, was instituted by Mr. Genet for the express purpose of dissension, and to draw a line between the people and the government, after he found that the officers of the latter would not yield to the hostile measures in which he would embroil them. . . . . Can anything be more pernicious to the peace of society than self-constituted bodies, forming themselves into permanent censors, and under the shades of night resolving that acts of Congress are illegal and unconstitutional? Such declarations, after Congress, the legally

constituted legislative body of the country, had duly considered and discussed any law are," he continues, "well calculated to disturb the public tranquillity." He further informs Mr. Ball that these societies proclaim that all who "vote contrary to their dogmas are actuated by selfish motives, or under foreign influence, nay, are traitors to their country." In his speech to the two Houses of Congress, after the suppression of the revolt in Pennsylvania, the President said: "Let the citizens determine whether it has not been fomented by combinations of men who, careless of consequences, have disseminated from an ignorance or perversion of facts, suspicions, jealousies and accusations of the whole government." To this part of the address the Senate thus responded: "Our anxiety, arising from the licentious and open resistance to the laws in the west counties of Pennsylvania, has been increased by the proceedings of certain self-created societies, relative to the laws and administration of the government; proceedings, in our apprehension, founded in political error, calculated, if not intended, to disorganize our government, and which by inspiring delusive hopes of support, have been instrumental in misleading our fellow-citizens in the scene of the insurrection." Washington afterwards wrote Mr. Jay that there could be no doubt in the mind of any one carefully examining the subject, that these clubs fomented and caused the insurrection, and, in another letter, predicted that, if not checked, *they would destroy the Republic.* These clubs were modelled after the anarchical Jacobin clubs of France. One of them, the Madisonian of Charleston, was formally recognized as an affiliated branch of the Jacobin Club of Paris. The motion for this recognition was made by Collot d'Herbois. These clubs, which were composed in great part of foreigners, and instituted by Genet for the purpose of involving the country in hostilities with England, which said Chief Justice Marshall, concealed, under the imposing garb of watchfulness over liberty, "designs subversive of all those principles which preserve the order, the peace and the happiness of society;" which took for their model the Jacobin Club of Paris, and were patronized by d'Herbois, who, in one day, slew fifteen hundred innocent persons; which, in the opinion of the President and the Senate, were responsible for the Whiskey Insurrection; which Washington declared would destroy the Republic; these clubs, Jefferson approved and sustained. So much was he attached to them, that when the President ventured in his annual speech to suggest the propriety of imposing some restraint upon them, he flew into a fury, and asserted that the President had attacked "the freedom of discussion, and *was guilty of an inexcusable aggression.*" After the death of Robespierre, the Convention expelled the Jacobin Club of Paris from its hall, and finally closed its doors. Mr. Monroe, then Minister at Paris, in the dispatch announcing this action of the Convention, expressed his approval of it. The suppression of the Paris club and Mr. Monroe's approval thereof, went far towards vindicating Washington's opinions respecting the Democratic clubs in this country. After the publication of Mr. Monroe's dispatch, they lost their influence and soon ceased to assemble. As Justice Marshall said, the death of the Jacobin clubs was "the unerring signal" of the death of the Democratic societies, so closely were they allied—they were nourished from the same fountain of fanaticism, and dried up at the same time.

12. He held that one generation has no power to bind the succeeding generation by law, or by contract. In a letter to Mr. Madison, dated September 6th, 1789, he sets forth his views on the subject in full. Here are some extracts

from the letter: "The earth belongs in usufruct to the living; it is self-evident that the dead have neither power nor right over it. The portion occupied by any individual ceases to be his, when himself ceases to be, and reverts to the *society*." "No man can by natural right *oblige the lands he occupied, or the persons who succeed him in that occupancy, to the payment of debts contracted by him.*" "The wife or children take the land free of debts." After some illustrations, he proceeds: "Then, no generation can contract debts greater than can be paid during its own existence." He computes that a generation at twenty-one years of age, can contract for thirty-four years; at twenty-two years of age, for thirty-three years, and so on. (This is a miscalculation or oversight, the time is much shorter, as will appear further on.) "On similar grounds, it may be proved that no society can make a perpetual constitution, or a perpetual law. Every constitution, and every law naturally expires at the end of thirty-four years," etc. The above theories were not youthful fancies, but settled convictions; for on June 24th, 1813, he writes to John W. Eppes: "Each generation has the usufruct of the earth during its continuance; when it ceases to exist, the usufruct passes on to the succeeding generation, free and unencumbered, and so on, forever." "Each generation," he thinks, "is a distinct nation," with no right to bind the succeeding generation, " more than the inhabitants of another country." "At nineteen years, then, from the date of a contract, the majority of the contractors are dead, and the contract with them." In a letter to Dr. Gem, he revises the computation made in the letter to Madison, and thus concludes: "Then, *the contracts, constitution, and laws of every society become void in nineteen years from their date.*" On September 11th, 1813, he says, in so many words, that the State is not bound to pay the debts of a preceding generation. From the foregoing, it would appear that Jefferson wished to introduce a sort of general Statute of Limitations, based on what he called natural justice, which would outlaw every obligation, private and public, at the expiration of nineteen years from its date, and annul every law after the lapse of nineteen years from its enactment. As by the laws of nature, the majority of men of legal age is replaced by a new majority of such men every nineteen years, no national or private contract, he taught, was valid beyond that length of time. This means that each generation shall inherit from its predecessors all the benefits and advantages of their skill, wealth, knowledge, and industry, but take none of their debts, burdens, or obligations, a doctrine which not only evinces a strange lack of gratitude, but is repugnant to both common sense, and common honesty. No wonder that Jefferson, in communicating this theory to Mr. Eppes, stated that the letter was for his eye only.

13. Having reached the advanced position, that newspapers without governments are preferable to governments without newspapers, Mr. Jefferson had but a single step to take in order to attain the summit of political wisdom. This exalted position he assumed, when he thus wrote to Mr. Carrington: "Those societies, (as the Indians) *which live without government* enjoy, in their general mass, an infinitely greater degree of happiness than those who live under the European governments. . . . *Among them, public opinion restrains morals as powerfully as laws ever did anywhere.*"— *Letter of January* 16*th*, 1787.

Here is a precious collection of political whimsicalities. Were it possible to reduce them to practice, they would destroy organized society, and substantially prevent the establishment of government among men. But what else than whimsicalities could be expected from one who proposed for the new States to be formed from the Northwest territory, the following names: Michigania, Chersonesia, Metropotamia, Pelispia, Polypotamia, and Assenisipia? Though bold in speculation, Mr. Jefferson was irresolute, almost timid, in action; he shrank from a trial of most of his political theories. When he had an opportunity of testing some of his peculiar notions of government, he scarcely attempted to do so. Much of his reputation is due to the fact, that during his two Presidential terms, he made few innovations on the established order of things, but administered public affairs pretty much as they had been administered by the men whose measures he had denounced, and whose motives he had aspersed.

Hamilton characterized Jefferson as "a man of sublimated and paradoxical imagination, entertaining and propagating opinions inconsistent with dignified and orderly government." The words "sublimated and paradoxical" aptly describe his imagination, and, to a certain extent, are applicable to his whole mind.

The more his theories of government are examined, the more clearly will it appear that he was a mere tyro in statecraft. He wandered in the vast and prolific field of political economy, and, like a child, plucked here and there a flower that pleased him, but he was almost entirely ignorant of the wise legislative husbandry, which causes that field to yield rich harvests of national strength and prosperity.

CHAPTER XI.

ARE HIS "*ANA*" RELIABLE?

Mr. Jefferson's own statements respecting them, raise doubts of their reliability. Three of these statements are as follows: 1. "Twenty-five years or more from their dates, I have given the whole a calm revisal:" 2. "Some of the informations I had received, are now cut out from the rest, because I have seen that they were incorrect or doubtful, or merely personal or private:" 3. "I should not, perhaps, have thought the rest worth preserving, but for the testimony against the only history of the period, that pretends to have been compiled from authentic and unpublished documents." These statements are found in the prefix or preface to the *Ana*.

1. The revision was made in 1818, which date is but twelve years after the last entry in the *Ana*. In 1818, Jefferson was 75 years of age, and, therefore, not likely to have a clear recollection of what happened a quarter of a century previously. 2. The chief value of such writings as the Ana, is attributable to the fact that they are a sort of record of current events, made at the time they transpired, by one who participated in them. Transactions in which Mr. Jefferson took part, he certainly could relate more correctly at or about their dates, than he could *twenty-five years* afterwards. He hardly revised the copies of his opinions, or the documents filed with them. A revisal of his reflections on certain men, or of his opinions of others, is not very important. 3. The *Ana* were preserved for a cer-

tain purpose, namely: To testify against Marshall's *Life of Washington*. It is known that Jefferson, besides being politically opposed to Marshall, heartily disliked him on account of his rulings in Burr's case, and that the ex-President's party-prejudices were strong. Another statement, made in the prefix, is shown to be entirely incorrect, by a simple examination of the *Ana* themselves. The statement is that they contain copies of official opinions, submitted while Jefferson was in the cabinet, with "sometimes the documents in the case," and notes of transactions pertaining to his official duties as Secretary of State, whereas, they contain not only such papers as are mentioned, but his opinions of some of the prominent men of his period, anecdotes of others, accounts of cabinet meetings, incidents of the time, notices of events that occurred while he was Vice-President, and of some that happened when he was President. Seven pages are devoted to Aaron Burr. All the entries respecting him are dated after Jefferson left the cabinet. In the prefix, it is recorded that John Adams " was for two hereditary branches of government, and one honest elective one." On July 29th, 1791, Adams wrote Jefferson. " If you suppose that I ever had a design, or a desire of attempting to introduce a government of Kings, Lords and Commons, or in other words an hereditary Executive, or an hereditary Senate either into the government of the United States, or of any individual State, you are wholly mistaken." When the prefix contains such errors, can reliance be placed upon the *Ana* themselves? How much that was correct, did the revision eliminate? How much that was incorrect, did it insert? How much was originally doubtful? Under the date of January 26th, 1804, the *Ana* contains an account of an interview of Aaron Burr with Jefferson. In it, he states that Burr "began by recapitulating rapidly that he had come to New York a stranger, some years ago," etc. Mr. M. L. Davis, in his *Memoirs of Burr*, commenting on this entry asks: "Now, who that knows the history of Colonel Burr's life, will believe one sentence, or one word of this statement?" Mr. Morse, in his life of Alexander Hamilton, characterizes the *Ana* as "A work as untrustworthy as it is interesting, a blunderbuss, which the aged man loaded to the very muzzle with garbled gossip, but carefully forbade to be discharged, until he himself had secured the safe refuge of the grave."

CHAPTER XII.

JEFFERSON AS GOVERNOR, IN TIME OF WAR.

In the year 1780, while the English officer, Leslie, was threatening an incursion into the state of Virginia, Jefferson, then Governor, thought of resigning his office. Edmund Pendleton, having heard of this, wrote to a friend " It is a a little cowardly to quit our posts in these bustling times." By a despatch, dated December 9th, Washington informed Jefferson that a large British force, supposed to have a Southern destination, was about to sail from New York. The course of military events, rendered it very probable that Virginia might at any moment be invaded. On December 29th, twenty-seven of the enemy's vessels entered the capes of Virginia, of which event Jefferson was next day apprised. The hostile fleet anchored at Jamestown, January 3d, 1781. On the 4th, a detachment of " 830 men and thirty horse," landed at Westover, and set out for Richmond, which they reached on the following day. Notwithstanding the notice, and the probability that an invasion was imminent, there was no force ready to oppose their advance. There seems to have been no effort, even to ascertain the plans or watch the movements of the invaders, who were commanded by Arnold. All the available militia having been ordered to Williamsburg, where they were useless, Arnold met with no resistance. He marched from Westover to Richmond, a distance of twenty-five miles, " without receiving a single shot."

The Legislature dispersed at his approach, the Governor

deserted Richmond under cover of night, and the city was thus left entirely at the mercy of the traitor. The Governor, charged with the defence of the State, and having reason to expect an invasion of it, made no defence,—fled from its defence. He admitted to Washington that "no opposition was in readiness." The commander-in-chief, through Hamilton, answered: "It is mortifying to see so inconsiderable a party committing such extensive depredations with impunity." Arnold seized the public stores at Richmond, destroyed the cannon foundry and burned a large quantity of tobacco, as well as many public and private buildings. General Henry Lee, in his *History of the Southern War*, says respecting this invasion: "It will scarcely be credited by posterity that the Governor of the oldest State in the Union and the most populous, should have been driven out of its metropolis and forced to secure personal safety by flight, and its archives with all its munitions and stores yielded to the invader, with the exception of a few, which accident, rather than precaution, saved from the common lot. Incredible as the narrative will appear, it is nevertheless true." After stating some of the injurious results of the Governor's flight, the General exclaims: "What ills spring from the timidity and impotence of rulers! In them, attachment to the common cause is vain and illusory, unless guided in times of difficulty by courage, wisdom and concert."—Vol. ii., pp. 6–14.

Henry Lee, in his *Observations*, p. 133, says Jefferson "never faced the enemy, nor even observed him, and until he ascertained that Arnold had retreated to his ships, kept himself behind the current of a broad and unfordable river, flitting from place to place, hiding his guns to protect them from the 'heavy rains.'" In a letter to General Muhlenberg, the Governor unwittingly exposes the incompetency or the neglect of some one, by stating that Arnold, on his march to and from Richmond, might have been captured " with facility by men of enterprise and firmness." There were assuredly many such men in the State. Why were not some of them sent to capture him? Whose duty was it to send them? After Arnold had returned to the fleet, Jefferson began to experience a strange longing for his seizure. It was this longing that prompted him to address the letter to Muhlenberg, to whom he further writes: " It is above all things desirable to drag him from those under whose wing he is now sheltered." It really seems that Jefferson, for the time being, believed that the capture of Arnold was the most desirable of all military achievements. He certainly evinced more interest in regard to that, than he appears to have shown in regard to the defence of his native State. He asked General Muhlenberg to select for the capture men from " the Western side of the mountains," and gave him minute directions as to the projected enterprise, some of which can scarcely be read without a smile. " The smaller the number," he remarks, " the better, so that they may be sufficient to manage him. Every necessary caution must be used on their part to prevent a discovery of their design by the enemy." He wished them to be informed that " their names will be recorded with glory in history with those of Van Wert, Paulding and Williams," and undertook to give them, if successful, five thousand guineas. This plan for the seizure of Arnold having failed, Jefferson devised a second one, in which he expected to have the assistance of Washington himself, and the whole French fleet. This magnificent scheme also proved abortive. When Arnold quitted the state, Cornwallis entered it. As the Governor had been occupying his own time, and wasting that of army officers with his fanciful schemes for seizing a single individual, Virginia was no better prepared to resist Cornwallis than she had been to repel the invasion of Arnold. In this extremity, Jefferson appealed to the commander-in-chief to come in person to defend his "own country." The appeal was in vain. Tarleton raided through the state at his pleasure, and came very near capturing the Governor, who made his escape from Monticello about ten minutes before the arrival of the foe.

In 1780, Virginia had a militia of fifty thousand, thirteen thousand of whom had their homes adjacent to the seat of war. These men were not deficient in soldierly qualities. The soil of the state was productive, the climate genial. The Legislature had invested the Governor with extraordinary powers, and was ready to sustain him in the exercise of still greater power, should the public exigencies render it necessary. This was shown by the large vote in favor of a dictatorship. Many of the inhabitants were wealthy. How did Jefferson avail himself of these unusual advantages for the successful discharge of the duties devolving upon him? We have seen that while he was Governor, his state was utterly powerless to repel even the small force commanded by Arnold. The veteran Steuben, then stationed in Virginia for the purpose of collecting and forwarding reinforcements to General Greene, and at the same time aiding in her defence, was indignant that nothing was done to check the advance of that force. He reported that there was not a man, except those sent by himself, to oppose the progress of the invaders. He complains that the recruits gathered by him were not supplied with arms, declaring that even those at Richmond were sent away in such haste, on the approach of the enemy, that they could not be found. After repeated requisitions, made in vain, he ventured to suggest to the Governor that men without arms could only consume provisions. He lacked camp-kettles and tents, and recommended that some one be appointed, whose duty it should be to collect the scattered tents of the State. In one of his official letters, he stated that with all his importunities, he did not think he would have been able to equip a certain body of troops in six weeks, had not stores arrived from the Northward; and that " nothing can be got from the State rather *for want of arrangement, than anything else.*" In another, he asked to be recalled on account of his "ill success." When General Greene first saw the Virginia recruits, at Charlotte, December 6th, 1780, he wrote Jefferson: " Your troops may be said to be *literally naked*, and I shall be obliged to send a considerable number of them away until they can be furnished with clothing. . . . . No man will think himself bound to fight the battles of a State that leaves him to *perish for want of clothing.*" General Muhlenberg reported that he had two thousand men in camp, with but three hundred muskets, and that it was "derogatory to the honor of the State," that a mere handful of invaders should be suffered to remain so long within her borders, but, *that without arms,* he could do nothing. In a letter to Washington, dated February 10th, 1781, the Governor admitted a deficiency of 3188 men in Virginia's quota of troops.

Why is it that in the years 1780, and 1781, Virginia, with her wealth, population, and resources, neither repelled hostile inroads upon her own territory, nor furnished her full contingent of troops to the Continental army? That she sent her men into the field poorly equipped and half clad? Baron Steuben indicated the answer to these questions, when he reported that it was "rather for want of arrangement than anything else." Her Governor was deficient in executive ability; he was a good word-monger, but in action he failed. He asked Congress "particularly to aid us with cartridge-paper and boxes, the want of which, small as they are, renders our stores useless." What insufficiency does this reveal? Were there no persons in Virginia capable of making these "small" articles? If not, why were not competent men brought from the Northern cities?

Besides his want of executive ability, he was hampered by a sensitiveness, verging on timidity, that caused him to shrink from incurring the odium, that might result from a proper enforcement of the laws for putting Virginia in a state of defence. Money was essential for any effort in that direction—it was not forthcoming. Jefferson admitted that it could be obtained by force, but hesitated because that, as he said, was "the most impalatable of all substitutes." The laws empowered him to impress horses for the military service; they were numerous in the State, but most of them belonged to the planters, whom Jefferson did not venture to offend, and the impressment languished. In consequence of this, when Cornwallis entered Virginia, he readily possessed himself of about a thousand fine horses. Thus, animals, that should have been employed in the service of the State or of the country, were, by mal-administration, reserved for the use of the enemy. The troops which Tarleton sent forward in advance to capture the Governor at Monticello were, most probably, mounted on some of these very animals. Had he been taken prisoner, and escorted to British headquarters by men riding upon horses just seized by the enemy in Virginia, the event would have been a rude, but not entirely undeserved reminder of neglected duty. In answer to those who imputed to him inefficiency at this period, the Governor pleaded that he was "unprepared by his line of life and education for the command of armies."

Prescott, Knox, Howard, Lee, Greene, were not bred to arms, yet they and others, without a military education became distinguished officers in the war of the Revolution. But it was not necessary that he should "command armies." No one blamed him for declining to perform such service. It is admitted that many excellent men are utterly unsuited for military operations, and, no doubt, he was one of them. As Governor he should have encouraged, stimulated, and directed the citizens; he should have pointed out the advantages to the common cause that would result from courage, energy, and activity, and the damage that would be inflicted upon that cause by indolence, apathy, and illiberality. He should have sought counsel of the best soldiers and the best civilians; he should have been diligent in season and out of season; vigilant in observing the movements of the foe; careful that the management of every department of the public service was intrusted to the person best suited to administer it. He should have seen to it that the recruits were properly organized, armed, equipped, fed, and clothed, and made as comfortable as circumstances would permit, while in the State; he should, have despatched as rapidly as possible those of them destined for the Continental army. These and similar duties were devolved upon him, in those stirring times, by his official position. It will hardly be asserted that he thoroughly performed any of them; some of them he scarcely attempted to discharge. For example, Steuben writes Washington: "Since the Virginia line was detailed to the Southern army, it was never regularly formed, nay, since I have been in the United States, it has never had a regular organization." But it is said that the voice of accusation in regard to these matters should be silenced by the exculpatory resolution of the Virginia Legislature. Let us see. After the raid of Arnold,

George Nicholas preferred charges against the Governor, touching his conduct and management of affairs during the raid. Owing to the dispersion of the Legislature, they were not then acted upon. At the next session, a committee was appointed, November 26th, 1781, " To state any charges, and receive such information *as may be offered*, respecting the administration of the late Executive." It will be perceived that the committee was not authorized to make any investigation. In the meantime, Jefferson had received a copy of the charges, and been elected to the House of Delegates. Soon after the organization of the House, he rose and stated that he was now ready to answer every accusation that might be brought against him. Mr. Nicholas was not present. No one spoke. Jefferson then read the charges against himself, or, more properly, the interrogatories which had been propounded to him in regard to his official action during the period mentioned above, and also the answers to them which he had prepared. There was no reply. The committee having reported that " no information being offered on the subject, except rumors, their opinion is that the rumors are groundless;" the House, and subsequently the Senate, passed a resolution, not only exculpatory, but laudatory. A resolution thus passed was not a vindication —not an acquittal. How could there be an acquittal on certain charges, when there had been no investigation as to their truth or falsity? The mere *ipse dixit* of the accused was accepted as a full answer to them. The issue of these proceedings may be accounted for on other grounds than a conviction of Jefferson's non-culpability. The surrender of Cornwallis, on October 19th, a few weeks before the report of the committee, removed all apprehension of other desolating invasions. It was the harbinger of peace. All hearts were aglow with the expectation of long-deferred independence. It was an era of good feeling. Why disturb the universal joy, by a prosecution that could accomplish no good? Why bring reproach upon a distinguished citizen, whose renown was part of the renown of the State? Moreover, a vote of censure upon the Executive, under the circumstances, would have been a reflection upon the Commonwealth and its citizens. Possibly, too, some of the legislators who favored the resolution exculpating Mr. Jefferson, were prompted to this action by feelings similar to those of the Jews, who went out of the Temple one by one when the Saviour said: "He that is without sin among you, let him first cast a stone at her." It is hardly to be expected that legislators, who had four times adjourned and dispersed at the approach of the enemy, would very strongly condemn the Governor for being somewhat disconcerted by the proximity of the same disturbing cause.

Though his friends assert that the resolution is a vindication, the whole proceeding was very unsatisfactory to Jefferson himself. His reply to Mr. Monroe, who urged him to be present in the Assembly at its next session, shows his shame and humiliation, and admits his consciousness of public condemnation. In this reply, he writes, May 20th, 1782: "Before I ventured to declare my determination to withdraw from public employment, I considered that I had *even lost the small estimation* I had before possessed." He could have borne the disapprobation of the people, he says, but that of their representatives was a shock on which he had not calculated. "But in the meantime," he continued, "I had been suspected in the eyes of the world, without the least hint . . . being made public, which might restrain them from supposing that I stood arraigned for treason of the heart, and not merely weakness of the head; and I felt that these injuries had inflicted a wound on my spirit which will only be cured by the all-healing grave." It is not the "integrity" of Jefferson that is here in question, nor is it his "ability," both of which are lauded in the resolution; it is his inefficiency of which complaint is made. The evidence of this inefficiency is too strong to be brushed away by any resolutions of a sympathizing assembly, least of all by a resolution adopted under the circumstances above detailed. Some of this evidence has been presented. Here is more. Colonel Meade, a Virginian, who had been on Washington's staff, but who was in his native State when Arnold made his incursion, declared that it was a "shame" that the traitor escaped so easily. In regard to that event, the Colonel further wrote: "The misfortune, in the present invasion, was that in the confusion the arms were sent everywhere, and no timely plan laid to put them into the hands of the men who were assembling." General Greene, towards the close of 1780, writes: "The numerous militia which have been kept on foot (in Virginia) *have laid waste almost all the country*, and the policy, if persisted in, must in a little time, render it almost impracticable to support a regular body of troops sufficient to give protection and security to the State. The expenses attending this business in the waste of stores exceeds all belief." General Steuben, having selected four hundred picked men as a reinforcement for General Greene, was surprised at receiving a paper "signed by the officers, complaining of the *ill-usage by the State*, and of the distressed condition of officers and men, and concluding that until something was done for them, they would not think of marching." These men were the "best provided" of Muhlenburg's corps.—*Steuben's Letter of December 4th*, 1780.

On December 18th, the Baron informs the commander-in-chief that, although many of the "abuses," which kept so many men from the field, had been abolished in the Northern army," in the Virginia line they *have reached their highest pitch*. . . . The officers do not care for the soldiers, and they scarcely know the officers who have to command them. . . . This State, having only a handful of regulars in the field, is continually ransacked by bands of officers and soldiers, who are drawing pay and rations for doing no service at all, *while they are committing excesses everywhere.*" In May, 1781, Steuben complains that "only two men have been employed by the State for the reparation of arms since January." On May 23d, Lafayette, then in Richmond, writes to Hamilton: "General Greene has directed me to take command in this State. It then became my duty to arrange the departments, which I found in the *greatest confusion and relaxation;* nothing can be obtained, and yet expenses are enormous. . . . Government wants energy, and there is nothing to enforce the laws." On May 5th, General Greene reported that the two thousand men promised to him from Virginia, and anxiously expected, were still delayed, and expressed fears, based upon information received, that but few of them would in the end join him. Later, the same General wrote to Jefferson himself: "The tardiness, and finally the countermanding the militia ordered to join this army, have been attended with the most mortifying and disagreeable consequences." For the actual "countermanding" Jefferson is not responsible, but he is responsible for the shameful tardiness, without which it would not have been possible.

In March, 1781, there were in General Muhlenberg's camp but eight rounds of ammunition to each man, and provisions for four days. Towards the end of May, the discontent of the public mind with the existing state of affairs became so serious, that the project of a dictator for

Virginia was defeated in the Assembly by only a few votes. Would nearly all the members of the Legislature have concurred in the opinion that such an extraordinary expedient was necessary, if the government of the State had heretofore been properly administered? If no blame attached to him who then was Governor, if he had done all that was possible under the circumstances, if his past official conduct had inspired confidence, why did not they who favored a dictatorship, recommend that he be entrusted with unlimited power? Why was the name of Patrick Henry on the lips of the people? No one thought of Jefferson for the post. Mr. Girardin says: "To introduce this officer, it was necessary to place Mr. Jefferson *hors de combat.*" Mr. Randall, his biographer, states that "all the misfortunes of the period were charged upon him" (Jefferson). On June 3d, Steuben reports that the men under his command, over five hundred in number, had neither shoes nor shirts; that they were *perishing in the wilderness without sufficient clothing to permit them to drill;* that he had received arms from Philadelphia, but not a cartridge-box or a saddle was in store; that he did not believe a single article of either kind could be procured in Virginia, though the first is as essential to a foot-soldier as the last is to a mounted man, and he had several times given notice that they were required. Mr. Wirt (*Life of Patrick Henry*) states that the period under consideration was one of "*almost hopeless darkness,* when the energies of the State seem to have been pretty nearly paralyzed."

Such was the condition of the proud and populous Commonwealth at the end of Jefferson's two years' administration. It cannot be said that her resources had been consumed by the fires of war, for she had hardly begun to be the theatre of military operations. Her condition was traceable to other causes. The impotence mentioned by Lafayette, the negligence, mismanagement, and other "abuses," of which Steuben, that faithful and energetic soldier, had often, but vainly complained, had done their work. The prediction of the sagacious Greene in regard to a certain policy was verified.

Mr. Jefferson appropriately closed his gubernatorial career by retiring to Monticello, and virtually abandoning the government, at a time when charges against him for official misconduct were pending, and when, in the language of Mr. Benjamin Harrison, "an implacable enemy was roaming at large in the very bowels of the State." When Jefferson, as Governor in time of war, is compared with some of the famous "War Governors" of our day, his inferiority strikingly appears.*

---

* For some facts and references in this note, the writer is indebted to Hamilton's *History of the Republic*.

CHAPTER XIII.

HIS INDIRECTNESS.

Rietiimüller, in his *Life and Times of Hamilton*, states that Jefferson, when a boy at school, was in the habit of putting forward other boys to ask for what he wanted. This indirectness, this desire to avoid personal responsibility, which characterized the child, was apparent in the man. Though he organized and long controlled a great political party, he never mounted the hustings to explain or defend its tenets: he issued no pamphlets or open letters; he contributed no article to magazine or newspaper in advocacy of his own doctrines, or in refutation of those of his political opponents. Mr. Hildreth, in his history, rightly observes that Jefferson was, perhaps, the only prominent man of his time, who "never touched pen to paper for the political enlightenment of the contemporaneous public." The brilliant success which he achieved for himself and his party, was won by the agency of others. He was the most skilful political "wire-puller" of his day. But he was much more. He was an efficient organizer; he possessed great tenacity of purpose. The stirring words, too, which he addressed, through his subalterns, to his adherents, were bugle-calls to battle. He so finely portrayed the beauties and the blessings of Republicanism, so strongly denounced those friends of monarchial institutions who, he pretended, were striving to overthrow it, that the hearts of his partisans glowed with enthusiasm for the good cause, and with indignation against its enemies.

He might with propriety have been styled the commander-in-chief of the Republicans, but for the fact that he never appeared at the head of his forces. When Hamilton, over the signatures of "Metellus" and "An American," pointed out the inconsistency of a man's remaining a prominent member of an administration, whose measures he was opposing, Jefferson called upon Mr. Madison to reply. This fact, standing alone, would excite no surprise, for Jefferson was well aware that, in an open controversy, he was no match for his great rival, whom he calls "a colossus to the anti-Republican party," and "a host within himself." It is, however, strange, that he made no answer to any of the personal attacks upon himself in the press, which were both numerous and bitter. He either induced some one else to repel such assaults, or vented his wrath in letters to friends, and awaited a convenient opportunity for punishing the offender. No private or political reasons overcame his resolution not to appear in the newspapers. The publication in this country of the Mazzei letter, which every one attributed to Jefferson, seemed imperatively to demand a public explanation from him, but none was made. He was most hostile to the Jay treaty, earnestly desired to prevent its ratification; but instead of writing strong articles in opposition to it, he entreated Madison "for God's sake take up your pen, and give a fundamental reply to Curtius and Camillus."

The pen of this gentleman, over whom he acquired great influence, was often invoked, and several times placed at his service.

Jefferson did not meet his political foes face to face in

manly combat. He assailed them in private letters, to be used by those to whom they were addressed. In these letters, he rarely attempted to show that the dogmas of the Federalists were erroneous, or to expose the fallacy of their arguments. He hurled epithets at them; ascribed to them unworthy motives and ulterior designs; or charged them with actual misconduct. So cautious was he, that these imputations and charges were seldom made in direct terms. They were involved in circumlocution, suggested, insinuated. In this prudent work of insinuation he excelled; it was congenial to his nature.

He could blast a man's character in a letter with such subtlety, that with the paper before you, you could scarcely point out a specific sentence to denounce as false or slanderous. A passage in one of his letters to Washington, referring to Hamilton's objection to the appointment of Freneau as translator in the State Department, will serve as a specimen of Jefferson's insinuated slanders. He therein declared that he never could have "imagined that the man who has the shuffling of millions backwards and forwards from paper into money, and money into paper, from Europe to America, and America to Europe; the dealing out of treasury secrets among his friends in what time and manner he pleases, and who never slips an occasion of making friends with his means," would have founded a charge on the appointment mentioned. Jefferson's life furnishes some remarkable instances of shrinking from responsibility for one's own opinions. Having drawn up the Resolutions of 1798, he communicated them to Mr. Nicholas, with the request, that the name of the author should not be revealed. When he wrote his famous letter to Dr. Rush respecting religion, he desired the Doctor not to give it publicity.

When he imparted to Madison his wild theory of a general bankruptcy, and a recommencement of national financial operations every nineteen years, he urged Madison to promulgate it as his own, because he occupied a high "station in the councils of his nation," and intimated that his fine logical powers might win for it popular approbation.

CHAPTER XIV.

JEFFERSON AND GENET.

The official conduct of Mr. Genet, while Minister to the United States, is probably without a parallel in the history of diplomacy. He abused the President, and openly expressed disdain of his authority. He intimated that Washington, in his course towards the French ambassador, was instigated by foreign influence, told him that in a certain contingency he should have awaited the action of Congress; declared that he had in several instances transcended his powers—that he did not represent the people; charged him with violating the laws of his country, the law of nations, and the treaties of the United States. He gave instructions to the President respecting his duties, and on the interpretation of international law. He asked the discharge, at once, of the whole debt owed by this country to France, which was, by agreement, payable in instalments. When informed that such payment was impracticable, Genet greatly incensed, retorted that this refusal *"tended to accomplish the infernal system* of the king of England and of the other kings, his accomplices, to destroy by famine French freemen and French freedom," and that our government was guilty of "a cowardly abandonment of their friend, France, in her hour of danger." He complained that he "had met with nothing but disgust and obstacles in the negotiations with which he had been charged." He threatened forcible resistance should the United States attempt, in a certain matter, to assert their supremacy over their own territory.

He informed the President that his country was indebted to France for its independence.

There was in his official communications an assumption of superiority, peculiarly offensive. His insolence reached its climax in a letter to the Secretary of State, dated July 25th, 1793, wherein he thus writes: "In vain *does the thirst of riches preponderate over honor* in the political balance of America. All this condescension, all this humility ends in nothing; our enemies laugh at it. And the French, too confiding, are punished for having believed that *the American nation had a flag—that they had some respect for their laws,* some conviction of their strength, *and entertained some sentiment of dignity.*" Such an insulting document was never delivered by an ambassador to the government to which he was accredited. Genet did not offend in words alone. His acts were, if possible, characterized by more arrogance and audacity than his letters. Soon after his arrival at Charleston, he began fitting out in our seaports privateers, to prey upon the commerce of Great Britain, a nation with which we were at peace. Without asking permission, he established in our maritime towns pretended Courts of Admiralty, presided over by French consuls, for condemning and selling as prizes, English or Spanish vessels, captured by the cruisers of France. He enlisted men, native and foreign-born, to serve under the flag of his country, posting in various cities, even in the Federal capital, placards calling for recruits for the French army; he issued some three hundred blank commissions, as invitations to Americans to man privateers or enter the French navy. He organized secret clubs, to aid him in his nefarious measures, and persuade our people to sympathize and coöperate with him in his opposition to the government. He attempted to arm and equip within our borders, expeditions for the invasion of Florida and Louisiana. When reminded by the President that these proceedings were contrary to the comity of nations, and some of them positive violations of international law, as well as of our own laws, he replied that he was familiar with these laws, and the President was mistaken; this too, although Vattel states that "The man who undertakes to enlist soldiers in a foreign country, without the sovereign's permission, violates the most sacred rights of the prince and the nation. This crime is punished with the utmost severity, in every well-regulated state. Foreign recruiters *are hanged without mercy.*" Finding remonstrance in vain, the President began to take action proper to vindicate the sovereignty of the nation. Upon this, Genet threatened to ignore the legally constituted authorities, and appeal directly to the people.

The despatch of the Little Democrat to cruise as a privateer, was the most outrageous transaction of Genet. This vessel, originally British, had been captured, brought into our waters, and condemned as a prize by one of his improvised Admiralty Courts. He bought her, changed her armament from two to fourteen guns, fitted her out, and commissioned her as a privateer. These things were done at Philadelphia, the capital of the nation, under the very eye of the government, in undisguised contempt of its authority, after he had been informed that such proceedings were offensive and not allowable. Jefferson saw Genet and asked him to delay the departure of the vessel until a certain day; he would make no promise, but said she would not be ready by the day indicated, thus leaving the impression that she would not sail before the time specified. The President extended international etiquette so far, as to express to Genet the wish that he would detain her until her case, and other similar ones, then under consideration by the cabinet, should be decided. Notwithstanding this condescension, on the part of Washington, Genet permitted the Little Democrat to put to sea, without according to our Executive the poor courtesy, due unasked, of awaiting an official examination of the important questions, legal and diplomatic, pertaining to her capture, sale, and new equipment. He did this, moreover, when he knew that the President had reason to believe from Jefferson's account of his interview, that the vessel would not sail before the time mentioned; when he was aware that assurances had been given to Great Britain, that the fitting out by the French in our harbors of privateers to operate against her merchantmen should cease, and at a time when he was detaining two English vessels, unlawfully captured, the restoration of which the President had demanded. But what cared he for the embarrassment that he occasioned the Government? His real purpose was to force this country into hostilities with England, and he was ready to employ whatever means were necessary to accomplish that purpose.

The state of affairs which Genet and his abettors had brought about in June, 1793, has been thus vividly depicted: "The United States presented an extraordinary spectacle. In each of their great seaports were seen tri-colored ensigns floating aloft above the American standards. French ships of battle moved so as to command their feeble batteries. The American coast lined with privateers plundering their unprotected commerce. Cruisers of their ally roaming on the high seas, commissioned to capture any neutral vessel freighted with the great staples of the country for their accustomed marts. An intestine party, banded together and rallying against their government, tendering homage to a foreign minister, after his known insults to the

President; that minister rebuking Washington as a violator of the laws, dictating to him his duty, appearing to divide with him the affections of the people; the cabinet in discord; the powers of the Chief Magistrate apparently ready to fall from his hands." Where stood Jefferson at this epoch? What was his attitude in this hour of his country's trial? Was he on the side of Washington, or on that of the French minister? Officially, as Secretary of State, he replied to the arrogant letters of Genet, and pointed out the illegality of his transactions in dignified and fitting terms. This he did, at the request of the President, but in the cabinet meetings, he opposed a demand for the restoration of vessels captured by privateers fitted out in our ports. He opposed the forcible detention of such privateers, after Genet had been notified that they must not put to sea; he opposed the publication of the correspondence between Genet and our government; he opposed the transmission of a statement of Genet's proceedings to Mr. Morris, to be laid before the French National Convention; he opposed the making of a demand for the recall of the obnoxious minister. In fact, he heartily favored none of the important measures, which were resorted to in order to check the mad career of this haughty and overbearing foreigner. There was one exception—he approved the Proclamation of Neutrality. He would have been more consistent had he opposed this also. After the proclamation was issued, Hamilton wrote a series of articles in explanation and defence of it, whereupon Jefferson entreated Madison to answer Hamilton and attack it. Madison thus urged, attacked both the form and substance of the proclamation, *that the Secretary of State had approved in the cabinet.*

When Washington received Genet coldly, he repaired to Jefferson, who listened patiently to the story of his alleged grievances, and to his complaints against those ungrateful, unworthy Americans, who hesitated to jeopardize everything in aid of a sister Republic; endeavored to sooth and pacify him, professed to be his friend, talked to him, no doubt, of tyrants and aristocrats, of equality and fraternity, and sent him away encouraged to persevere in his evil ways. The Democratic journals, too, espoused his cause. The *National Gazette*, Jefferson's mouth-piece, took the lead in this unpatriotic work. It declared that the French minister was "*too accomodating* for the sake of the peace of the United States." In one of its articles, respecting enlistment in the French service, was the following violent passage: "Thanks be to God, the sovereignty still resides with the people, and neither proclamations, nor royal demeanor and state can prevent them from exercising it." Another article proclaimed that Genet had as much right to appeal to the people as the President had; that his interpretation of our treaty with France was as good as the President's, and that the people must ultimately interpret it. The key-note of this French music, performed on Jefferson's organ, was struck by himself in a private letter to Madison, written in April, when Genet's advent was expected. The minister's arrival, he wrote, would " furnish occasion for *the people to testify their affection without the cold caution of the Government.*"

Such, for some time, was the course, and such the attitude of Jefferson, and of those under his influence, towards the man, who again and again " flung full defiance in the face " of the administration, of which Jefferson was prime minister; who, as he himself tells us, was " disrespectful, even indecent to the President " (*Letter to Madison, July 7th*), and who had committed offences, the penalty of which, according to Vattel, was death. And when, at last, he assented to the demand for Genet's recall, this assent was given not because Genet's conduct to Washington had been "indecent," not because he had contemned the authority of the government, and trampled upon the law of nations, not because he had in his letter of July 25th insulted the whole American people, or because he had endeavored to embroil us with England, but because the rising flood of public indignation against the minister threatened to overwhelm the Democratic party, and, with it, the Secretary of State.

When it was noised abroad that the impudent Frenchman had insulted Washington, and even intended to disown entirely the government of which he was the head, the affection of the people for their venerated President manifested itself in an unmistakable manner. Jefferson quickly trimmed his sails for the popular breeze by cutting loose from Genet, and acquiescing in a measure which, theretofore, he had stoutly opposed. In a confidential letter to Madison, dated August 11th, he says: "I believe it will be true wisdom in the Republican party to approve unequivocally of a state of neutrality, to avoid little cavils about who shall declare it; to abandon Genet entirely, with expressions of strong friendship and adherence to his nation, and confidence that he has acted against their sense. In this way, we *shall keep the people on our side* by keeping ourselves in the right. . . . I adhered to him *because I knew what weight we should derive to our side*, by keeping in it the love of the people for the French cause and nation. Finding at length that the man was incorrigible, *I saw the necessity of quitting a wreck, that would sink all who should cling to it.*"

The motive that prompted Jefferson to adhere to Genet, and to desert him, was apparently the same, a desire to promote the success of his party, and not concern for the public welfare. The letter asking the recall of Genet was an able and convincing paper, severely arraigning him for his misdeeds. When he learned that Jefferson was the author of it, he was much angered, and addressed to the Secretary a spirited epistle. In it he stated that certain persons in the United States, often mentioned to him as royalists, opponents of popular rights, and Anglo-men, had determined to thwart him in his laudable effort to unite the two Republics in resistance to tyrants, by demanding his recall. He upbraided Jefferson, for permitting himself to be the generous instrument of these enemies of liberty, in their designs against him, " after he had pretended to be his friend, after he had initiated him into mysteries, which have inflamed his hatred against all those who aspire to arbitrary power." He said, further, that if he had expressed his desires and purposes to the American Government with too much boldness, he had thus erred because " it was not in his character to speak, as many people do, *in one way, and to act in another; to have an official language, and a language confidential.*"

CHAPTER XV.

JEFFERSON AS A DEMAGOGUE.

One of the peculiarities, that distinguished Jefferson from most of the prominent men of his time, was the zeal with which he pursued popularity. Some of his eminent contemporaries doubtless prized highly the respect and esteem of their fellow-citizens, but Jefferson, more assiduously than any of them, employed the means best calculated to win the favor of the multitude. Though the assistance received by this country from France during our Revolution, was rendered by King Louis XVI., at his own royal will and pleasure, Jefferson, after he began his quest for popularity, always spoke of our debt of gratitude to the French people, as if they, and not the King, had aided us in our hour of need and peril. He complained that Washington, in his dress, equipages, and receptions, assumed the trappings of royalty, and denounced these things as unrepublican. He wished all ceremony at the "Executive House" discontinued; he seldom rode in a carriage, except on long journeys—that mode of conveyance was too aristocratic; he went to his inauguration on horseback, and humbly hitched his own horse.* He was ever flattering the people, praising their purity and their good sense, prating about their rights, and charging with a design to invade their liberty, men

---

* *Travels for four and a half years, in the United States,* by John Davis. London, 1803.

who had achieved that liberty, while he was begging their help, or fleeing from the enemy. He insisted that Washington, Hamilton, and others were intent upon establishing a monarchy, while he and his followers, especially himself, were engaged in a desperate struggle against such a perversion of the government, thus inducing the ignorant masses, for ignorance was then general, to believe that he was their defender and champion, ever battling to save them from the tyranny of a king, from being thrust back into the thraldom, from which they had just been delivered. How adroit, and how unprincipled! He led the people to believe, too, that the Federalists were attempting to thwart "the popular will." He accused Hamilton of corruption in office, pretended he was under British influence. He said that all titles, including *Excellency*, *Honor*, *Worship*, the harmless *Esquire*, even the unoffending *Mister*, were inconsistent with Republican simplicity, and should be abolished. He perceived the superiority of the English Government and institutions of his time over those of France. He well knew the impurity of the social life of the French; he was convinced that there was little domestic happiness among them, that conjugal love was blasted by the fires of passion, that in consequence of the prevailing corruption, the education of young Americans in France was not desirable, and wrote these facts to his friends; but he persuaded the people that he was the special admirer of everything pertaining to France, and thus availed himself of American affection for that country. Observing the popular antipathy to royalty, he execrated kings and monarchies in general, and wished them swept from the face of the earth. Yet he recommended the continuance of royalty in France. He said that most of the European nations were unfit for popular government, but raged against the slightest tendency to kingly authority, or any appearance thereof in this country. In this way, he played upon the self-love of his fellow-citizens by implying that *they* were fit for a democratic government, and secured their votes.

The following extract from a letter to Mr. Gerry, of Massachusetts, will illustrate Jefferson's method of flattering the multitude, and depreciating the leaders of the party opposed to him: "But the people will rise again. They will awake like Samson from his sleep, and carry away the gates and posts of the city. You, my friend, are destined to rally them again under their former banners. The people will support you, notwithstanding the howlings of the ravenous crew from whose jaws they are escaping. It will be a great blessing to our country, if we can once more restore harmony and social love among its citizens. It is almost the first object of my heart. *With the people* I have hopes of effecting it. But their *coryphœi are incurables.* I expect little from them." Instead of discouraging the unreasonable hatred of England, entertained by the vulgar, he endeavored to turn it to account, by insulting the British envoy, Mr. Merry. That gentleman had not in any manner wronged him; and merely as a well-bred stranger, to say nothing of diplomatic etiquette, was entitled to courteous treatment. But on the occasion of his formal presentation, by the Secretary of State, to Jefferson, then President, the latter received him in slippers down at the heels, with coat, pantaloons, and undergarments indicative of utter slovenliness, and indifference to appearances—in a state of negligence, that seemed actually "studied." This Mr. Merry states in a communication to Josiah Quincy. One can imagine how this reception of the British minister, as well as Jefferson's designation of all kings as "vermin," delighted the populace of that time. Finally, he taught that insurrections should be lightly dealt with, lest the people be discouraged in their efforts to maintain their liberties. By such devious ways, and such ignoble devices did Mr. Jefferson court popular favor. In view of them, "Tom" Moore can almost be pardoned for writing of him:

> "Inglorious soul,
> Which creeps and winds beneath a mob's control,
> Which courts the rabble's smile, the rabble's nod."

CHAPTER XVI.

JEFFERSON AND BURR.

On June 17th, 1797, Jefferson wrote to Aaron Burr as follows: "Perhaps some general views of our situation and prospects, since you left (Philadelphia), may not be unacceptable. At any rate, my letter will give me an opportunity of recalling myself to your memory, and of evidencing my esteem for you." On December 15th, 1800, Jefferson thus addressed him: "I feel most sensibly the loss we sustain of your aid in our new administration. It leaves a chasm in my arrangements which cannot be adequately filled. I had endeavored to compose an administration whose talents, integrity, names, and dispositions, should at once inspire unbounded confidence in the public mind, and insure a perfect harmony in the conduct of the public business." He concludes this letter with "affectionate salutations." His esteem for Burr had now ripened into affection. On February 1st, 1801, he sent Burr a manuscript missive in regard to a letter alleged to have been written by Jefferson to Judge Breckenridge, in which were expressions highly injurious to Burr. In this missive, he pronounces this alleged letter a forgery, declares that he never wrote to the Judge a sentiment unfriendly or disrespectful to Burr, and, again assuring the latter of his esteem and respect, warns him against those wicked men who would "sow tares between us." He closes in these terms: "A mutual knowledge of each other furnishes us with the best test of the contrivances which will be practiced by the enemies of us both." These extracts from Mr. Jefferson's letters leave no doubt as to his opinion of the person to whom they were addressed. From them we learn that he esteemed, respected, and admired Burr; that he confided in his integrity; that their relations were those of friends. On turning to Jefferson's *Ana,* we find under date of January 26th, 1804, these entries: " I had never seen Colonel Burr till he became a member of the Senate. His conduct soon inspired me with distrust. I habitually cautioned Mr. Madison against trusting him too much." " He was always at market, if they had wanted him." On April 20th, 1807, Jefferson wrote his friend, William B. Giles: " I never, indeed, thought Burr an honest, frank-dealing man." There is certainly a surprising, not to say startling, contrast between Jefferson's three letters to Burr, and the private memoranda above cited; between what Jefferson wrote to Burr, and what he wrote of Burr. It may be alleged in explanation of this contrast, that the memoranda were made three years after the date of the last letter to Burr, and that, in the interval, Jefferson had, for sufficient cause, changed his opinion in regard to Burr's character. This explanation will not avail for two reasons: *First.*—When Jefferson wrote to Burr the letter last mentioned, they had been acquainted for ten years, since Burr entered the Senate in 1791. As Jefferson was Secretary of State while Burr was Senator, and as they belonged to the same political party, it is almost certain that they were frequently thrown together. An acquaintance of ten years, under such circumstances, must have enabled each to form a pretty accurate estimate of the other's character. *Second.*—Jefferson, in the *Ana,* states that he began to distrust Burr soon after the latter became Senator, and from the letter to Mr. Giles, we learn that Jefferson *never* thought Burr an honest, frank-dealing man. It appears then, from Jefferson's own writings, that he entertained the same opinion of Burr when he wrote the three letters, as he did when he made the entry in the *Ana*. How shall Mr. Jefferson escape from the dilemma of self-contradiction, in which his letters to Burr, his *Ana*, and his Giles letter place him? Did he really purpose calling to his cabinet, as one of his confidential advisers on great questions of national policy, a man, upon whom he habitually cautioned one of his friends not to place too much reliance? Did the sage of Monticello indeed feel an affection for one whom he never thought honest? Did he wish to secure and preserve the friendship of a person whom he distrusted? Or were all these professions of esteem, and regard, and affection insincere, and intended merely to secure the aid of Burr's talents and influence in promoting the success of Jefferson's own schemes? That they were so intended, may be inferred from the circumstances under which the letters to Burr were written, from their language, from the habits of the writer, and from the political history of the time.

A brief examination of these letters, in connection with the entries in the *Ana*, respecting Burr, and with Jefferson's subsequent treatment of him, will reveal some of the methods employed by Jefferson in the management of his personal and party interests, and thus throw light on his real character. Note that Jefferson was not in the habit of writing to Burr; indeed, it is not a little remarkable, that the three letters mentioned are the only letters to him found in Jefferson's published correspondence, voluminous as it is. Note that neither of them was written in reply to a verbal or written communication from Burr, or at the instance of another person. Note that the first letter begins with a wish to be recalled to Burr's recollection, and to express esteem for him. It is not unreasonable to suppose that a letter opening thus, and written on the writer's own motion, to one with whom he had never before corresponded, indicates the writer's desire for some favor from the person so addressed. Was there, in this case, a favor desired? And if so, what was it? When the letter was written Jefferson was Vice-President under John Adams, President, whom it was generally believed a Republican would succeed. Jefferson was a very prominent Republican. He had been mentioned as a candidate for the succession. He had aspirations for the Presidency. As early as 1794, he wrote to Mr. Madison of "double delicacies" on that subject, which had prevented him from expressing himself freely to the latter. He knew that the electoral votes of New York were almost indispensable to secure his election. He knew also that Burr was the man most powerful in controlling those votes. He was, of course, anxious to secure the coöperation of one so influential, in advance of all competitors. Under these circumstances, he penned the first letter to Burr, flattering him, inquiring particularly after his health, expressing serious apprehensions for the safety of " our Republican Government," and indirectly asking a reply, by expressing the wish that he could give the writer some solution of his " painful and doubtful questions," concerning the dangers that menaced the Republic. Can it be doubted that this letter was written for the purpose of obtaining Burr's assistance in mounting to the chief magistrate's chair? To one familiar with Jefferson's correspondence and methods, it seems most probable, that he hoped and expected Burr to reply that the "questions" would be solved by the elevation of the Vice-President to the Presidency.

Now as to the second letter, dated December 15th, 1800. In the preceding November, there was an election for Presidential electors. The Republican candidates were Jefferson and Burr. The Federalists voted for Adams and Pinckney. By the Constitution, as it then was, the person who received a majority of the whole number of electoral votes was the President, but, "if there be more than one who have such a majority, and have an equal number of votes, then the House of Representatives shall immediately" choose one of them for President. Jefferson had reason to believe that he and Burr had each received a majority and an equal number of votes, and that the election must devolve on the House. In such case, a coalition between the Federalists, and the Republicans who favored Burr, would result in his election, provided he acquiesced in the arrangement.

How important, then, for Jefferson to ascertain the views and purposes of the man who might defeat or elect him, or at any rate, to conciliate that man! More than three years had elapsed since a letter had been received from or written to Burr by him, though he was an indefatigable letter writer. Now, however, he favored his long-neglected friend with one of his caressing epistles. This letter is truly Jeffersonian. It is confidential. It is sent by private hands, and not by mail, lest in "this prying season," as Jefferson called it, some one besides Burr should read it. Seemingly frank, it is really disingenuous. In it there is no hint of a possible election by the House, which Jefferson feared, nor does he directly state that he had been chosen President, and Burr Vice-President. But he makes a calculation from which it appears that such is the fact. Assuming it to be so, he congratulates Burr on his election, and expresses the belief that such a result is more gratifying to him than any appointment by the Executive. He then modestly alludes to the talents, the integrity, the reputation of some one, without positively saying that Burr is talented, upright, and renowned, though the words used seem to imply all this. He flatteringly alludes to the loss "we sustain of your aid in our new administration," intending to convey the impression that he proposed appointing Burr a member of his cabinet, in case of the latter's non-election to the Vice-Presidency, but carefully abstaining from an explicit declaration of such purpose. (Was the assumed election of Burr really a surprise to Mr. Jefferson?) The letter concludes with "affectionate salutations." When the character of this letter, its date, the long interval between that date and the date of the preceding letter, the political situation, and the peculiar relations of Burr and Jefferson, resulting from the failure of the electors to elect a President, are considered, the motives that prompted Jefferson to write the letter of December 15th, are manifest. The third letter, penned not long after, evidences greater solicitude than either of the others for the friendship of a certain person who was always in the market, for it was then certain that the election had devolved upon the House, and it had been bruited about that Burr was willing to accept an election by the united votes of Republican and Federal members.

After repeated ballotings, Jefferson was chosen by the House of Representatives on February 17th, 1801. Elevated now to the summit of his ambition, and sustained by an ever-increasing popularity, he no longer had need of Burr's assistance, and addressed to him no more adulatory letters.

On the evening of January 26th, 1804, Burr called upon Jefferson. In the course of their conversation, Burr mentioned the growing distrust of himself by the Republican party, and adverted to the attacks upon him by the press.

He then said that as his term of office as Vice-President would soon expire, he would be somewhat compensated for this distrust and these attacks, if he could return to his home with some evidence of the President's undiminished confidence in him. In this connection, he recalled to Jefferson's recollection his letter of December 15th, 1800, in which he mentioned his purpose of appointing Burr to his cabinet. The President agreed with Burr in condemning the journalistic assaults upon him, but added that these attacks no more influenced his opinion of Burr than the passing wind. Their conversation then turned upon other topics. Nothing occurred during the interview, to indicate any change in the cordial relations heretofore existing between the President and Vice-President. At parting, the subject of the appointment was left to the consideration of the President. *On that very evening* Jefferson wrote down in his *Ana* the disparaging sentences respecting Burr, above quoted.

This statement might well be doubted, were its truth not established by the *Ana* themselves. In March, 1806, Burr several times visited Jefferson. The *Ana* mention three of these visits. During one of them, Burr again asked Jefferson for an appointment. The President, in reply, expressed his admiration for Burr's talents and his belief that Burr, if called to any place in the government, would use his fine abilities for the public welfare, but declined to appoint him upon the ground that he had lost the confidence of the people, and that the President had determined to place in office no man who did not possess that confidence. Burr subsequently dined with the President, and again called to take leave of him, before quitting Washington.

Whether the motives above ascribed to Jefferson for writing the three letters to Burr were, or were not the motives that really prompted him to write them, these letters, his *Ana*, and his letter to Mr. Giles, above mentioned, taken together, clearly reveal his insincerity. It is not a single instance of duplicity which is brought to light by these writings, but insincerity extending through more than a decade of years, and apparently systematized. It would seem, too, that during much of this time, he was practicing a double deception; he was deceiving Burr and deceiving the public, since Burr's, dining at the White House and his several calls on the President, all undoubtedly noised abroad, were well calculated to diffuse the idea of their continued intimacy.

The insincerity was attended with aggravating circumstances. Without solicitation, Jefferson offered his friendship to Burr, and in three successive letters, he expressed his admiration and respect for him; he manifested much solicitude to retain his friendship. During the interview of 1804, he talked and acted as if his feelings towards Burr were unchanged, yet almost immediately after his guest had departed, he wrote in his private note-book that he had entertained a distrust of that guest, and a belief in his venality, long before the three letters to him were written. After having penned this secret indictment of the man whose friendship he had courted, and while it still remained uncancelled, Jefferson several times received Burr at the Presidential mansion, complimented him on his talents, expressed his confidence that those talents, if opportunity were offered, would be employed for the good of the country, entertained him at dinner, and again permitted his guest to depart, without an intimation that he had lost the President's friendship, or that there had been any diminution of his regard. May not the man who can act thus, be reckoned an adept in dissimulation?

Asssociated with Jefferson's insincerity in dealing with Burr, is his flattery of the latter, a flattery so fulsome that it may almost be styled sycophantic. He thrusts himself on the attention of Burr. He writes one letter in order that he may have an opportunity of recalling himself to the memory of Burr, and of evidencing his esteem for him. In another, he eulogizes Burr's abilities, integrity, disposition, popularity, and assures him that his election to the Vice-Presidency, leaves a chasm in his (Jefferson's) new administration, "which cannot be adequately filled." Although Burr made no reply to either of these letters (none is found in the published correspondence of either Burr or Jefferson), when the latter heard of his alleged letter to Breckenridge, he did not wait for any complaint on the part of Burr, but hastened to write the obsequious letter of February, 1801, which is as follows:

"DEAR SIR:
"It was to be expected that the enemy would endeavor to sow tares between us, that they might divide us and our friends. Every consideration assures me that you will be on your guard against this, as I assure you, I am strongly. I hear of one stratagem so imposing, and so base, that it is proper I should notice it to you. Mr. Mumford, who is here, says he saw in New York before he left it, an original letter of mine to Judge Breckenridge, in which are sentiments highly injurious to you. He knows my handwriting, and did not doubt that to be genuine. I enclose you a copy taken from the press copy, of the only letter I ever wrote to Judge B—— in my life; the press copy itself has been shown to several of our mutual friends here. Of consequence, the letter seen by Mr. Mumford must have been a forgery, and, *if it contains a sentiment unfriendly or disrespectful to you*, I affirm it solemnly to be a forgery, as also, if it varies from the copy enclosed. With the common

trash of slander, I should not think of troubling you, but the forgery of one's handwriting is too imposing to be neglected. A mutual knowledge of each other, furnishes us with the best test of the contrivances which will be practiced by the enemies of both. Accept assurances of my high respect and esteem."

No man with true nobility of soul will play the sycophant to the most excellent of his fellow creatures, but Jefferson flatters and fawns upon one, whom he pronounces venal and unworthy of confidence. We have said that the dissimulation of Jefferson towards Burr was apparently systematized. We mention three of the facts which suggested this reflection. 1. Jefferson knew Burr, nearly *thirteen years*, before he wrote in the *Ana* his opinion of him. 2. Burr, in referring to the letter of December 15th, did not distinctly remember its date. Jefferson took the pains to find the letter, to write down its precise date in his account of the interview, and to state in that account, that he intended to appoint Burr to a place in the cabinet, in consequence of his party services and political success in New York, reasons, it will be perceived, somewhat different from those mentioned in the letter. 3. We find in the *Ana* no entry between the memorandum respecting Burr's first interview, dated January 26th, 1804, and the memorandum regarding the second, dated April 15th, 1806, which Jefferson says was made about a month after the interview, and which, be it noted, is the last entry in the *Ana*.

Whatever may have been Jefferson's opinion of Burr during the earlier years of their acquaintance, it is certain that he later conceived a strong hatred of him. This hatred, concealed for a time, manifested itself conspicuously, just before and during Burr's trial for treason in 1807. In that trial, Jefferson exerted his personal and official influence to secure a conviction. He was not content to trust the prosecution to Mr. Hay, the U. S. District Attorney, assisted by the splendid talents of William Wirt, but practically assumed its control, and wrote letter after letter containing directions as to its management. So eager was he, that he diregarded in this matter official dignity and propriety; he hunted up evidence, he named certain witnesses whom he wished to be summoned—he himself conversed with a number of persons in order to ascertain what would be their testimony, if placed upon the stand; he sought to procure convicting evidence by urging upon one of the accused a pardon, unsought, and once refused; he descended to petty details, such as directing Mr. Hay, in what manner to examine a particular witness; he actually requested that officer to *send him subpoenas for witnesses.*

Having stooped from the high office of President to perform the functions of an assistant public prosecutor, he seems to have descended still lower. Shortly after Burr's trial, Dr. Erick Bollman, the friend of Lafayette, published an account of what passed between himself and Jefferson in reference to the case. In that account, the Doctor sets forth that he voluntarily called upon the President, and in the presence of Mr. Madison, made to him a statement of what he knew respecting the transactions for which Burr was soon to be tried; that Jefferson soon after, wrote him a note in which the President asked him to commit to writing what he had stated at their recent interview, and gave his word of honor that the statement should never be used against the Doctor, or permitted to pass out of Jefferson's hands; that in a letter, delivered to the President, he made the statement desired; that Mr. Hay admitted in open court that he had that letter, but refused to deliver it to the foreman of the grand jury, who had asked for it; that it further appeared in court, that General Wilkinson had seen in Hay's possession a letter to the President signed by Bollman, and finally, that the doctor had still in his possession Jefferson's note containing his request and solemn promise abovementioned, a copy of which note appears in the published account.

Three of the doctor's allegations, to wit: that he wrote a statement respecting Burr's case, that it was delivered to Jefferson, and was subsequently in the possession of Mr. Hay, are proven by a letter from Jefferson to Hay, transmitting a written statement of Dr. Bollman touching the case, (there could hardly have been two such statements), and authorizing the District Attorney to use it against the Doctor, should he greatly prevaricate in his examination before the grand jury. It is possible that Jefferson never wrote the note which Bollman avers he did write, and a copy of which is embodied in the doctor's publication, but it is almost incredible that the Doctor made statements the falsity of which could so easily be shown. If the note was penned or dictated by Jefferson, he undoubtedly violated one of the promises it contained, and authorized the violation of the other in a certain contingency.

Jefferson's animosity to Burr extended itself to his counsel, and to the tribunal before which he was tried. He criticised the rulings of the judges, pronounced some of them contrary to law, and endeavored to inspire Mr. Hay with distrust of the court of which he was an officer. He informed Mr. Giles that the testimony " will satisfy the world if not the judge (Marshall) of Burr's guilt," and wickedly charged that great jurist and pure man with trying to shield Burr from merited punishment. He styled Burr's leading counsel, Luther Martin, " an unprincipled and impudent

Federal bull-dog," and asserted that all Burr's most clamorous defenders were his accomplices. He asked Mr. Hay whether " we shall move to commit Luther Martin as *particeps criminis* with Burr." The letter containing this suggestion is a painful revelation of Jefferson's malignity towards Burr, and all who ventured to defend him. He proposed to deprive a man on trial for his life, of the assistance of that counsel most familiar with his case and best qualified to defend him, as well as of the active sympathy of a devoted friend, when friends were few; to pain Mr. Martin by preventing him from defending his friend in the direst emergency, to humiliate him by arresting him while engaged in the trial, to fix a stigma upon a renowned and honorable advocate, by thrusting him into jail upon the charge of participating in a great crime. Jefferson cannot be excused for suggesting this monstrous proceeding—a proceeding without precedent in the history of criminal prosecutions—upon the ground that he had discovered evidence sufficient to convict Martin. He hints at no such evidence. All he hopes to do is to fix upon Martin " a *suspicion of treason.*" He adds: " at any rate his testimony (that of a newly-found witness) will put down this Federal bull-dog." His professed reasons for proposing the committal of Martin were, that he had been informed that it was generally believed in Baltimore that Burr was planning an unlawful enterprise of *some sort*, that Luther Martin knew all about this enterprise, and that he (Jefferson) had received a letter stating that one Graybell could possibly prove this knowledge. It will be perceived, that he does not claim to have information that Mr. Martin had aided or abetted the " conspiracy " for which Burr was on trial, or had any knowledge of it, or that he had entered into any illegal combination whatever, and that the suggestion of a committal was made before it had been ascertained by actual examination or otherwise, that Graybell could testify to the commission of any improper act by Martin. For no better reasons than these Jefferson was willing, apparently, to inflict the cruel wrongs above mentioned upon two gentlemen, his peers, one of whom had not only been a Senator and Vice-President of the United States, but had received the same number of electoral votes for the Presidency as Jefferson himself; the other of whom had sat in the Convention which framed the Federal Constitution, and, at the time of the contemplated outrage, was one of the most eminent lawyers of the country.

Burr's acquittal on the charge of treason did not appease, but apparently augmented Jefferson's wrath. He indirectly charged somebody (name suppressed in letter) with endeavoring to clear Burr, and "keep the evidence from the world." In order to prevent the latter calamity, he absurdly and tyranically directs Mr. Hay not to pay the witnesses, or permit them to depart, until their testimony delivered at the trial is reduced to writing. He further directs Mr. Hay to obtain a copy of the record of the trial and of the judge's opinion, *without saying for what*, and to send them, with the evidence, all duly certified, to him at Washington. He orders the trial of Burr for misdemeanor. Forgetting or disregarding the fifth Amendment to the Constitution, he desires Mr. Hay to consider whether Burr cannot be again tried in Ohio for treason, after the misdemeanor trial is ended either by conviction or acquittal. Burr's case had twice been before a grand jury in Kentucky, and had each time been dismissed; he had been tried for treason at Richmond, and acquitted. Jefferson had already directed his prosecution for misdemeanor, and now hopes that he may be imprisoned for this offence, so that "we" may have time to decide whether his former friend shall again be placed in jeopardy of his life, and exposed to an infamous death. Well might General Jackson denounce Jefferson as a "persecutor" of Burr, and Luther Martin declare that Jefferson hunted Burr, "with a bloodhound's keen and savage thirst for blood."

Jefferson's indignation at Burr's acquittal is further shown by his indirect but bitter assaults upon Judge Marshall. Writing to Mr. Hay, he says: "This criminal is preserved to become the rallying point of all the disaffected and worthless of the United States." The following from one of his letters to General Wilkinson, one would suppose to be the production of a bedlamite, rather than of the President of the United States: "The scenes which have been acted at Richmond are such as have never before been exhibited in any country, where all regard to public character has not yet been thrown off. They are equivalent to a proclamation of impunity to every traitorous combination which may be formed to destroy the Union." With that vagueness of expression that he could so well employ, he suggests an amendment to the Constitution "which keeping judges independent of the Executive, will not leave them so of the nation." In this, as in other cases, he vents his indignation by covert attacks in letters to friends. His parting shot at the Judge was sending to Congress a copy of the proceedings, the evidence and the Judge's charge at the trial of Burr.

Although Jefferson strove to obtain a conviction of Burr for the crime of treason, it is doubtful whether he really believed him guilty. In a letter to Mr. Giles he sets forth the transactions of Burr, upon which he bases the charge of treason. These are: 1. "The enlistment of men in a regular way. 2. The regular mounting of guard round Blennerhasset's Island, when they discovered Governor Tiffin's men to be on them. 3. The rendezvous of Burr with his men at the mouth of the Cumberland. 4. His letter to the acting Governor of Mississippi holding up the prospect of civil war. 5. His capitulation regularly signed with the aids of the Governor, as between two independent hostile commanders."

It is hard to understand how a lawyer or even an intelligent and unprejudiced layman, who had read the Constitution, could decide that those transactions amounted to treason. Further, in a letter to Mr. Bowdoin, then our Minister at Madrid, Jefferson says: " Although at first he (Burr) proposed a separation of the Western country, and on that ground received encouragement from Yrujo, according to the usual spirit of his Government toward us, yet he very early saw that the fidelity of the Western country was not to be shaken, and *turned himself wholly towards Mexico.*" Mr. Schmucker, in his impartial biography of Jefferson, expresses the opinion that Jefferson's non-belief in Burr's guilt is evident from this letter.

Notwithstanding these letters, and other facts which may be advanced in support of the theory deduced from them, it is impossible to believe that Jefferson, insincere and unscruplous as he may have been, was base enough to procure the execution of a man of whose innocence he was persuaded. It is more probable that he endeavored to have Burr convicted, regardless of his guilt or innocence, with the intention of pardoning him. By his conviction for treason and his pardon, Jefferson could humiliate and ruin one who, he supposed, had intrigued to supplant him in his first presidential contest, and at the same time, blazon his own magnanimity to the world, that is the people, whose favor he courted with all the obsequiousness of a petty shop-keeper.

CHAPTER XVII.

JEFFERSON'S SLANDERS OF HAMILTON.

Some one has said of Jefferson: "He did not hesitate to attribute to them (his political opponents) purposes which no honest mind could form, and no rational mind entertain." This, if true, is not very flattering to the judgment of him whom it concerns, and still less so to his heart. A brief examination of some of the purposes and practices which Jefferson attributed to Hamilton, will enable us to form an estimate of the accuracy of the foregoing statement respecting him.

1. He alleged that Hamilton favored his friends and adherents, by communicating to them at opportune times the financial secrets of the Treasury. The charge is made in two letters to Washington, one dated May 23d, 1792, the other, September 9th, 1792. In this, as in other similar cases, he offered no proofs of the truth of his injurious allegations against a brother cabinet officer. The fact that he brought forward no evidence in support of the charge, evinces his inability to do so, for he certainly lacked not the inclination. But while there is nothing to establish its truth, there are strong reasons for believing it untrue. While Hamilton was Washington's private secretary, he contracted an intimacy with Henry Lee, then at the headquarters of the army. This intimacy ripened into friendship. Towards the close of 1789, while Hamilton was preparing his report on the public credit, Colonel Lee addressed him a letter, containing certain inquiries respect-

ing the fiscal measures which he proposed recommending to Congress. The information, which the colonel wished thus to elicit, he expected to use for his private pecuniary benefit. There was probably no one, whom the Secretary would have more willingly obliged than his quondam associate in arms. But mark his reply, found in Vol. V., p. 446, of his works: "My dear Sir; I received your letter of the 16th inst. I am sure you are sincere when you say that you would not subject me to an impropriety, nor do I know that there would be any in answering your queries. But you remember the saying about Cæsar's wife. I think the spirit of it applicable to every one, concerned in the administration of the finances of the country; with respect to the conduct of such men, suspicion is ever eagle-eyed, and the most innocent things may be misrepresented. Be assured of the affectionate friendship of yours," etc. This letter does not indeed prove that Hamilton never revealed treasury secrets to any one, but it raises the strongest presumption of his innocence. If he would not reveal them to one of his most intimate friends, in whose discretion he could certainly confide, and when by so doing he could strengthen his own Congressional influence, it may be safely inferred, in the absence of evidence to the contrary, that he did not impart those secrets to others. As Jefferson, though willing enough, adduced no testimony in support of his accusation, the conclusion is inevitable that his charge against the Secretary is false, and that the accuser had no reason to believe it true.

2. He charged that Hamilton wished the public debt "*never to be paid*, but always to be a thing wherewith to corrupt and manage the legislature." *Letter of Jefferson to Washington above mentioned, dated September 9th,* 1792, *Sparks Writings of Washington, Vol.* 10, Appendix. The evidence that this allegation is entirely unfounded,

and that Jefferson knew it to be so when he penned it, is as follows: On page 41, of Hamilton's Report on Public Credit, dated January 9th, 1790, is the following: "Persuaded as the Secretary is, that the proper funding of the present debt will render it a public blessing, yet he is so far from acceding to the position in the latitude in which it is sometimes laid down, that public debts are public blessings, a position inviting to prodigality, and liable to dangerous abuse, that he *ardently wishes to see it incorporated as a fundamental maxim in the system of public credit of the United States, that the creation of debt should always be accompanied with the means of its extinguishment.* This he regards as the true secret of rendering public credit immortal." He then proposes that certain revenues "shall be appropriated to *continue so vested until the whole debt shall be discharged.*" In Hamilton's Report on Estimates, he urges that a surplus of one million then in the treasury, should be applied to the discharge of the public debt. In his Report on Manufactures, bearing date December 5th, 1791, he says: "And as the vicissitudes of nations beget a perpetual tendency to the accumulation of debt, there ought to be, in every government, a perpetual, anxious, and unceasing effort to reduce that which at any time exists as fast as practicable consistently with integrity, and good faith." All these Reports were made and published long anterior to the date of the letter containing the charge; the first of them, two years and eight months before that date. This one was commented upon throughout the country, and as Jefferson reached home, on his return from France about the close of 1789, it may be safely assumed that prior to September, 1792, he had read the Report on Public Credit, and knew that one of the fundamental principles of Hamilton's financial system was that the extinguishment of a public debt should be provided for at the time of its contraction. If this report escaped his notice, it can scarcely be doubted that he was familiar with the Report of December, 1791, made when he was in the cabinet with Hamilton, and was impelled by both public and personal motives, to scan everything penned by the latter. Should this report, also, by any possibility, have been overlooked, Jefferson, as a member of the Cabinet, would necessarily learn the general principles upon which the Treasury Department was conducted. The proposition that Hamilton favored the payment of the public indebtedness is proven by official documents; the proposition that Jefferson wilfully misrepresented him on this point, is sustained by evidence, that will force conviction upon every one who examines it.

3. In immediate connection with the charge that has just been considered, is one of a much more serious nature, namely, that Hamilton wished the Public Debt "always to be a thing *wherewith to corrupt and manage the legislature.*" He elsewhere declares that Hamilton's financial system was "A machine for the corruption of the Legislature." He made no attempt to show that any one had been bribed or corrupted; he set forth no specifications. On February 28th, 1793, Mr. Giles, a friend of Mr. Jefferson, introduced into the House of Representatives nine resolutions touching Hamilton's alleged mismanagement of the Treasury Department. Two of them were abandoned—one of them was never voted on, and the remaining six were rejected by an average vote of about four to one. The inquiry set on foot by the resolutions, revealed Hamilton's integrity, and nice sense of honor. His enemies were greatly chagrined, and asserted that the resolutions had failed through the influence of members, interested in sustaining the Secretary.

The press continued its assaults upon him. At the next session of Congress, Hamilton demanded an investigation of the affairs of the Treasury. Resolutions in the nature of charges were preferred against him in both Houses. In the Senate, they were referred to a committee, and no further action is recorded. Two-thirds of the committee to which they were referred in the House, were Republicans. After a laborious investigation extending through a period of two months, this committee, on May 22d, 1794, made a report entirely exculpating Hamilton, which was adopted without a dissenting voice. This report, not only established the spotless purity of the Secretary, but bore testimony to his scrupulous obedience to the laws, as well as to his vigilance in guarding the public interests. Thus was Hamilton twice vindicated.

When it is considered that Jefferson made this charge against Hamilton while the latter was Secretary of the Treasury, and the former was Secretary of State; that the charge was made to the President, who was an intimate friend of Hamilton; that the reputation of Hamilton was unsullied, that the charges assailed the integrity of the legislature, as well as that of the Secretary; that the accusation asserted not one act only, but a system of corruption; that the accuser offered not a scintilla of proof in support of his terrible allegation, and that it was utterly false, it is scarcely too much to say, that a more shameful assault upon character is not to be found in the chronicles of slander.

4. In the letter, which contains the two preceding calumnies, Jefferson declared that Hamilton's career was "A tissue of machinations against the liberty of a country that had received and fed him." It is hardly necessary to say, that there was no attempt to sustain this sweeping accusation by any testimony, direct or circumstantial. The person who

made it, seems rarely to have thought it necessary to establish the truth of any defamatory statement respecting a political opponent, which he choose to put forth. He had repeatedly hinted, and indirectly preferred this charge, but had not before stated it clearly, or in such offensive language. Enough has been said in the Note on Jefferson's Apprehensions of a Monarchy, to show that it is unfounded. Even if nothing in disproof, could be brought forward, it must be regarded as false, for he, who speaks or writes what injuriously affects the character, or the interests of another, and fails to prove the truth of his declaration, is held, both in law and in reason, to have uttered what is untrue.

In addition to what has been stated in refutation of this accusation, two facts may be adduced. 1. In the Constitutional Convention Hamilton moved that the President be ineligible after two successive terms. See Hamilton's *History of the Republic*, vol. iv, chap. 72 and note. 2. In the *Ana*, under date of August 13th, 1791, Jefferson records that Hamilton, in a private conversation with him, condemned particularly Adam's " Davila," and, among other things, said : " Since we have undertaken the experiment, (of the present government) I am for giving it a fair course, whatever my expectations may be. At present, success seems more probable than it had done heretofore. . . . . That mind must be really depraved, which would not prefer the equality of political rights, which is the foundation of pure Republicanism, if it can be obtained consistently with order. Therefore, whoever by his writings disturbs the present order of things is really blamable, however pure his intentions may be." Here we have from Jefferson's own pen, strong if not sufficient testimony to disprove his allegation, for it is difficult, almost impossible, to believe that a man who spoke the words taken from the *Ana*, and whose sincerity is admitted by Jefferson himself, could be engaged in continual intrigues against the liberties of his country.

5. One more charge against Hamilton will be noticed. It is, that he not only favored a monarchy, but that *he wished "A monarchy bottomed on corruption."* This is assuredly a very remarkable accusation, but it is hardly more so than the evidence which Jefferson submits for the purpose of sustaining it. This evidence, found in the *prefix* to the *Ana*, is as follows: " But Hamilton was not only a monarchist, but for a monarchy bottomed on corruption. In proof of this, I will relate an anecdote, for the truth of which I attest the God who made me. Before the President set out on his Southern tour in April, 1791, he addressed a letter from Mount Vernon to the Secretaries of State, Treasury, and War, desiring that if any serious and important cases should arise during his absence, they would consult, and act on them. And he requested that the Vice President should also be consulted. This was the only occasion, in which that officer was ever requested to take part in a Cabinet question.

"Some occasion for consultation having arisen, I invited those gentlemen to dine with me, in order to confer on the subject. After the cloth was removed, and our question argued and dismissed, conversation began on other matters, and by some circumstance was led to the British Constitution, on which Mr. Adams observed, 'Purge that Constitution of its corruption, and give to its popular branch equality of representation, and it would be the most perfect Constitution ever devised by the wit of man.' Hamilton paused, and said, ' Purge it of its corruption, and give to its popular branch equality of representation, and it would become an impracticable government; as it stands at present, with all its supposed defects, it is the most perfect government that ever existed.' And this was assuredly the exact line, which separated the political creeds of these two gentlemen. The one was for two hereditary branches, and an honest, elective one; the other for an hereditary king, with a House of Lords and Commons, corrupted to his will, and standing between him and the people. Hamilton was, indeed, a singular character. Of acute understanding, disinterested, honest, and honorable in all private transactions, amiable in society, and duly valuing virtue in private life, yet so bewitched and perverted by the British example, as to be under thorough conviction that corruption was essential to the government of a nation."

Let this singular method of proving a statement be considered, for a moment. One gentleman imputes to another a certain theory as to government, but offers no proof in support of his imputation. He several times repeats it, and on each occasion, without evidence. Many years after, when the accused party had long been sleeping in his grave, the imputer, in order to sustain his charge, makes an entry in his diary. This entry contains what purports to be an account of an incident, that happened twenty-seven years before, to the accuracy of which the narrator makes the most solemn attestation; and also contains some reflections suggested by the incident related. The diary is not to be published during the life of its author. From the entry, it appears that an honorable man, "of acute understanding," was "so bewitched and perverted" by his admiration of the British Constitution, as to become thoroughly convinced "that corruption is essential to the government of a nation;" that a statesman, disinterested and honest in private life, favored "a House of Lords and Commons corrupted to his will, and standing between him and the people;" that a gentleman of more than ordinary intelligence, was stupid enough to avow, before persons, of whose friendship he was not assured, his preference of dishonesty to honesty in the administration of government. Is this senility? Perhaps it is; if so, it is a senility which makes no strong appeal to our sympathy; it is senility, engaged in a blundering attempt to transmit to posterity, a foolish calumny upon a pure and noble man, invented and propagated by its author, while in the full possession of mental vigor. The incident related by Jefferson, and its circumstances, deserve and will reward some attention.

Though this incident is remarkable in more than one respect, and apparently better worth remembering than many things set down in the *Ana*, there is no mention of it therein, and no record of it was made for more than a quarter of a century. When, in 1792, and at other times, Jefferson wrote to Washington and others that Hamilton favored a monarchy, and the latter attempted to repel the charge, this incident, the occurrence of which could have been proved by Adams, Knox, and Randolph, would probably have silenced him. When Jefferson imputed to Hamilton the purpose of using the public debt, to corrupt the Legislature, he might have imparted to this grave imputation upon the Secretary and upon Congress a certain plausibility, by citing the explicit declaration of the Secretary. When Adams denied that he desired a king, Lords, and Commons, and challenged Jefferson to mention some act or word that evidenced such a desire, reference could have been triumphantly made to the consultation dinner, which they had eaten together, a short time before. But the incident was recalled in none of these cases—not even in the last, where the temptation to do so must have been strong, and the task was easy. Armed with this double confession of political faith, the champion of Republicanism could have overwhelmed the two leading Federalists of his time. But, for some reason, he used this effective weapon in none of his contests.

Perhaps he did not avail himself of this "anecdote," in his party struggles, because the facts stated occurred at his own table; this delicacy cannot, however, account for his long delay in recording them. But why did he finally reduce them to writing? We may suppose that some such considerations as these moved him: " I have charged Hamilton and Adams with the design, and the effort to establish a Monarchy in this country. Both have strenuously contradicted the charge. I have offered no proof of my allegations. I have preferred a more serious accusation against Hamilton, but Congress has pronounced him pure in his high office. I shall soon pass away. The idea, that posterity may deem me capable of making false accusations against two of my most worthy and prominent contemporaries, is distressing to me. A circumstantial account of this consultation dinner will show to those who come after me, that my course towards these eminent men was not entirely without cause."

The time, at which the incident is stated to have occurred, though not precisely given, was scarcely three months before the date of Jefferson's letter to Adams, in which mention is made of their difference as to the best form of government. Was this mention due to Jefferson's recollection of Adams' post-prandial declaration? The latter, in his reply, makes no attempt to explain or qualify that declaration, as he would almost certainly have done, had he remembered it. Three facts are here to be noted: 1. This reply, in the ordinary course of the mails, would reach Jefferson but a few days prior to August 13th, 1791, the date of the *Ana* entry, which narrates Hamilton's condemnation of

Adams' writings, particularly "Davila." 2. This entry is the first in the *Ana*. 3. No other entry is made until the ensuing December. From the whole language of the entry, most of which is quoted above, page 139, and especially from its conclusion, one might infer that there is some relation existing between it, and the account of the after-dinner incident. Its conclusion is as follows: "This is the substance of a declaration, made in much more lengthy terms, and which seemed to be more formal than usual for a private conversation between two, and as if intended to *qualify some less guarded expression*, which had been dropped on former occasions. The inference would be strengthened by the fact, that this second declaration of Hamilton respecting governmental systems was made, as appears from a comparison of Jefferson's dates, only a few months after the first one was made. The account of the second seems to have been written in *August*, 1791; *the narrative of the first, in February*, 1818. Jefferson was, apparently, quite aware that posterity would deem it very extraordinary, that a man of Hamilton's character and understanding favored a "monarchy bottomed on corruption," but, at the same time, was most anxious to have it believed that such was the case, for he endeavors to account for the anomaly, and appeals to his Creator for the truth of his statements. That he was also unusually solicitous for the accuracy and reliability of his record of Hamilton's second declaration is clear, for he added at its close: "Thomas Jefferson has committed it to writing in the moment of A. Hamilton's leaving the room."

The incident at the consultation dinner so carefully recorded, and so solemnly attested by Jefferson, did not apparently impress Mr. Adams very strongly, as no mention of it is found in his writings,—indeed, he appears to have forgotten it in less than three months, although it is stated that it happened at the only Cabinet consultation which he attended while Vice-President. Mr. J. C. Hamilton, in his *History of the Republic*, avers that the incident could not possibly have occurred at the time stated, because at that period, in consequence of Cabinet disputes regarding the Bank question, the only intercourse between Hamilton and Jefferson was that of an official character, which was conducted in writing, and in the third person, and ridicules the idea that Hamilton made the declaration attributed to him. The narrator himself admits that his account of the incident was penned *twenty-seven years* after its alleged occurrence, and when he was seventy-five years old. Is it the dream of a dotard, or something worse?

CHAPTER XVIII.

JEFFERSON AND WASHINGTON.

The depravity of human nature is strikingly illustrated by the fact that the great and good man, to whom under Providence, this prosperous land is most indebted for the manifold blessings of independence, was, while yet alive, defamed by some of his own fellow-citizens. This is scarcely surprising, for the master-poet has said "Virtue itself 'scapes not calumnious strokes." But it is both astonishing and painful to discover among his detractors, the distinguished person who has occupied in popular affection the place next to that held by him, who is "first in the hearts of his countrymen;" it is astonishing to learn that Thomas Jefferson did not discourage, but possibly encouraged the calumniation of George Washington.

Jefferson's slighting allusions to this illustrious man began while he was Washington's Secretary of State. August 11th, 1793, he wrote Mr. Madison, "The President always acquiesces in the majority,"—that is, of the Cabinet. By thus writing, he not only endeavored to cast a slur on his chief, the President, but violated official propriety. In a letter to the same gentleman, dated December 28th, 1794, he wrote: "The denunciation (by Washington) of the Democratic societies is one of the extraordinary acts of boldness, of which we have seen so many from the faction of monocrats." He styles the denunciation "an attack on the freedom of discussion, the freedom of writing, printing, and publishing;" says that the President has taken advantage of the misbehavior of certain persons "to slander the friends of popular rights,"—that the President's proposition to restrain the licentiousness of these societies is "an abstract attempt (whatever that is) on the natural and constitutional rights" of these friends, and "an inexcusable aggression." In the same letter, referring to the then recent suppression of the Whiskey Insurrection, he alleges that the President in effecting that suppression, was guilty of "arming one part of the society against another,"—"of declaring a civil war, the moment before the meeting of that body, which has the sole right of declaring war," "of adding a million to the public debt;" he ridicules that part of the President's speech in which the reasons for calling out the troops are stated, and alludes to what he is pleased to term "the *fables in the speech*." In regard to the same subject, he writes to Mann Page, May 27th, 1795, "An insurrection was announced, and proclaimed, and armed against, and marched against, but none could be found." He concludes that the enforcement of the excise law by calling out the militia, will "make it the instrument of dismembering the Union, and setting us all afloat, to choose what part of it we will adhere to."

In one letter, he states that Washington was not sensible of the designs of his party; in another, to Madison, he describes him as "enveloped in the rags of royalty." Referring to Washington's approval of the Jay treaty, Jefferson says, "I wish that his honesty and his political errors may not furnish a second occasion to exclaim, 'Curse on his virtues, they have undone the country.'" In his letter to Aaron Burr, of June 17th, 1797, we find him lamenting Washington's "ungrateful predilection in favor of Great Britain." December 25th, 1796, he writes to Madison: "The President is fortunate to get off (his term would expire the coming fourth of March) just as the bubble is about bursting; .... he will have his usual good fortune of reaping credit for the good acts of others, and leaving to them that of his errors." Another letter of his to Mr. Madison, dated January 8th, 1797, contains this scandalous paragraph; "Monroe was appointed to office .... merely to get him out of the Senate, and with an intention to seize the first pretext for exercising the pleasure of recalling him." Writing to Mr. Tazewell, Jefferson thus expresses himself in regard to Washington, "I hope also that the recent insults of the English will at length awaken in our Executive that sense of public honor and spirit which they have not lost sight of in their proceedings with other nations, and will establish the eternal truth that acquiescence under insult is not the way to escape war."

The famous letter to Mazzei, dated April 24th, 1796, contains these passages: "The aspect of our politics has wonderfully changed since you left us. In place of that noble love of liberty and republican government, which carried us triumphantly through the war, an Anglican, monarchical, and aristocratical party has sprung up, whose avowed object is to draw over us the substance, as they have already done the forms of the British government. The main body of our citizens, however, remain true to republican principles." "Against us are the Executive, the judiciary, two out of three branches of the Legislature, all the officers of the Government .... and holders in the banks, and public funds, a contrivance invented for purposes of corruption." "It would give you a fever were I to name to you the apostates who have gone over to these heresies, men who were Samsons in the field, and Solomons in the council, but who have had their heads shorn by the harlot of England. We are likely to preserve the liberty we have gained only by unremitting labors and perils; our mass of weight and wealth on the good side is so great, as to leave no danger that force will ever be attempted against us. We have only to awake, and snap the Lilliputian cords with which they have been entangling us, during the first sleep which succeeded our labors." In this letter, Washington, who was the Executive when it was written, is accused of being a member of an Anglican, monarchical, and aristocratical party (a truly wonderful party, it may be remarked), whose avowed purpose is to establish here a government like that of Great Britain; a party, that has for years been "entangling the people for some ulterior purpose; that is so bent on the destruction of popular liberty, that it can only be preserved by "unremitting labors and perils:" he is charged with being an apostate, and with having approved and helped to create "a contrivance, invented for purposes of corruption." It is, moreover, intimated that he and his party meditated the employment of force against their political opponents, and that he is one of those whose head has been shorn by the harlot of England. It is true, none of these accusations are clearly formulated. Jefferson rarely made a direct charge, but they are none the less contained in the letter when it is read in the light of contemporaneous history.

Jefferson not only himself traduced Washington, but sanctioned, instigated, and probably procured the vituperation of him by others. The papers, that most violently assailed him and his administration, were the *National Gazette*, and the *Commercial Advertiser*, that afterwards became the *Aurora*. Washington wrote General Lee that the "publications in these two papers were *outrages on common decency.*" Two extracts from articles which appeared in them, when Washington's second term expired, show the character of their attacks upon him. *First.* "The man who is the source of the misfortunes of our country is this day reduced to a level with his fellow citizens, and is no longer possessed of the power to multiply evils on the United States. If ever there was a period for rejoicing, this is the moment. Every heart ought to exult, that the name of Washington from this day ceases to give currency to political iniquity, and to legalize corruption. A new era is opening, ... for nefarious projects can no longer be supported by a name. When retrospect is taken of the Washington administration, it is a subject of astonishment that a single individual could have cankered the principles of Republicanism in an intelligent people, and should have carried his designs against the public liberty so far, as to put in jeopardy its very existence; such, however, are the facts." *Second.* " If ever a nation was debauched by a man, the American nation has been debauched by Washington. If ever a nation was deceived by a man, the American nation has been deceived by Washington . . . . Let the history of the Federal Government instruct mankind, that the mask of patriotism may be worn to conceal the foulest designs against the liberty of the people." One is astounded at the audacity and malignity of these attacks.

Freneau, the editor of the *National Gazette*, was translating clerk in the office of the Secretary of State, and was appointed by Jefferson, whose *protegé* and dependant he was. Jefferson aided him in establishing his paper, recommended it to his friends, furnished it occasionally with public documents, and procured subscribers for it. It was universally recognized as the organ of the Secretary. During much of the time that Jefferson was a member of Washington's Cabinet, the *Gazette* kept up its abuse of the President, but the Secretary made no attempt to check it, and no apology to Washington for its denunciation of him.

The *Aurora* was under the control of B. F. Bache, who, educated in France, was fanatically favorable to the ideas of the French Revolution; Cobbett calls him, "That yelper in the Democratic kennel." He was a friend and admirer of Jefferson, whose claims to the presidency, he was one of the first to advocate. Jefferson urged Madison to obtain subscriptions for the *Aurora*, that at the time was languishing for lack of support. The *Gazette* and the *Aurora* advocated Jefferson's political sentiments, and expressed his opinion of the leading men of the time. In their editorials, there not infrequently appeared the turns of thought, and, sometimes, the very language found in his writings. In a sketch of Freneau, found in the *New American Cyclopædia*, it is said, that, according to Freneau's statement, the most severe attacks upon Washington's administration, which appeared in the *National Gazette*, " were written or dictated by Jefferson."

In addition to what has been stated respecting his immediate relations to these two papers, it may be said that after his retirement from the cabinet, Monticello became the headquarters of those opposed to Washington and his administration, and that Jefferson exercised all the prerogatives of the acknowledged leader of his party. Among those prerogatives was, of course, a large if not a controlling influence in the management of the whole party press. He must, therefore, be held mainly responsible for its virulent abuse of Washington.

A notorious libeller of the General, was James T. Callender, a Scotchman, who fled from Great Britain to avoid a prosecution. Having arrived in this country, he joined himself to the Republicans, and soon found congenial work in the publication of a scandalous attack upon Hamilton. While temporarily in charge of the *Aurora*, in the absence of Bache, he industriously slandered leading Federalists in its columns. He was subsequently invited by Mr. Mason, a Senator from Virginia, to his home near Alexandria. While sharing the Senator's hospitality, he was found drunk and dirty in the purlieus of a neighboring distillery. Arrested as a vagrant, and taken before two Justices of the Peace, he was committed to jail upon suspicion of having escaped from the Baltimore wheelbarrow gang. His host procured his release, by presenting his naturalization papers, and vouching for his good character. By the aid of Republican friends, he established the *Examiner* at Richmond. There, convicted of seditious libel for the publication of a pamphlet, entitled "*The Prospect Before Us*," containing slanders upon Washington and Adams, he was fined $250, and sentenced to nine months' imprisonment. This fellow complained that the honors accorded to the memory of Washington were idolatrous, and too expensive. Like Judas, when the weeping Mary poured the precious ointment on the feet of the Saviour, he asked, "Why was not this money given to the poor?"

Scarcely was Jefferson seated in the presidential chair, when he pardoned Callender, and by the exercise of a doubtful power, remitted his fine, which had been paid. He, moreover, five times sent him money;. three of these remittances were $50 each.

Incensed at his failure to obtain the Postmastership at Richmond, Callender ascribed to Jefferson the publication of *The Prospect Before Us*. Jefferson felt this keenly, styled Callender a "lying renegade," and promised to show the falsity of his imputation, by publishing all the letters he had ever written to him; but he never did so, alleging that the copies of them could not be found. Callender, however, produced the letters themselves, from which it appeared that Jefferson, notwithstanding his disclaimers to Madison and others, contributed money to defray the expenses of publishing the scandalous pamphlet, furnished information for it, and actually saw and approved some of the proof-sheets.

In an entry in the *Ana*, under date of August 2d, 1793, Jefferson states that General Knox, introduced into a Cabinet meeting a pasquinade on the President, in which Washington and others were depicted on a guillotine. The author of the *Ana* relates the occurrence, with perfect *sang-froid*, as if a brutal caricature of the President was no concern of his. He does not even express surprise; he characterizes what one must suppose was Knox's outburst of indignation at the outrage, as "a foolish and incoherent sort of a speech." He records with apparent satisfaction, that "the President was much inflamed—got into one of those passions, when he cannot command himself;" that he denounced that "rascal Freneau," and used improper language. But the narrator did not set forth the President's strong and frequent provocations to wrath, nor had he a word of censure for the author of the ferocious lampoon; the *enemies of Washington were the friends of Jefferson*. Jefferson's bearing towards the French minister, Mr. Genet, while the latter was insulting Washington and defying his authority, is noticed elsewhere.

In July, 1796, Thomas Paine addressed to Washington a letter, containing these passages: "When we speak of military character, something more is understood than constancy, and something more ought to be understood, than the Fabian system of doing nothing. . . . . The successful skirmishes, at the close of one campaign, make the brilliant exploits of Washington's seven campaigns. . . . . No wonder we see so much pusillanimity in the President, when we saw so little enterprise in the General, ... Elected to the Presidency, the natural ingratitude of your constitution began to appear.

The lands obtained by the Revolution, were lavished upon partisans; the interest of the disbanded soldier was sold to the speculator; injustice was acted under the pretence of faith, and *the chief of the army became the partner of the fraud.* ..... And as to you, sir, treacherous in private friendship, and a hypocrite in public life, the world will be puzzled to decide whether you are an apostate or an impostor; whether you have abandoned good principles, or whether you ever had any."

No one with an American heart, can even now read these words without indignation. Surely Mr. Jefferson had no connection, direct or indirect, with this infamous letter; surely, when it appeared, he hastened to denounce the insolent foreigner, who dared thus foully to insult a man, who was not only President of Jefferson's country, but his own friend. The letter was written at Paris, under the roof of Mr. Monroe, through whose intercession Paine had been released from a French prison. It is well known that Monroe was one of Jefferson's most intimate friends, more intimate with him, perhaps, than any one, except Mr. Madison. Jefferson subsequently wrote Paine a letter, of which this is the conclusion: "That you may long live to continue your useful labors, and to reap their reward in the thankfulness of nations, is my sincere prayer. Accept assurances of my high esteem, and affectionate attachment." After he became President, he gave Paine a passage from France to our shores in a national vessel, received him with honor at the executive mansion, and welcomed him to Monticello. It may be mentioned, that about the time Paine was set at liberty, Mr. Monroe declined to ask the discharge of Madame Lafayette from prison.

In order that the above-narrated transactions of Mr. Jefferson and his friends may be fully appreciated, the following facts should be considered. During the greater portion of the time over which the transactions extended, Washington was Chief Magistrate of the nation. He had rendered most valuable services to his fellow-countrymen, in war and in peace. His character was irreproachable. He was the most popular man in the country. He never wronged or insulted Mr. Jefferson, or even treated him with discourtesy —nor was he accused of doing so. He appointed Jefferson Secretary of State, honored him with his confidence, was his friend, when Freneau discharged his first poisoned arrow at the President, and remained his friend throughout the whole period of defamation. Jefferson knew full well that Washington was vexed and pained by the press attacks. This appears from the *Ana*, in which it is stated that he was "sore and hot" on account of them, and that on one occasion, he vehemently declared he would not continue to endure them for the empire of the world; it also appears from a letter of his to Jefferson, in which he complains with much feeling, that the denunciation poured upon him by the press, could be deserved only by "a Nero or a pickpocket."

He was vituperated at a time when he was beset with difficulties, and burdened with responsibilities, resulting from the changes effected in our civil polity by the Constitution —difficulties and responsibilities so great, that Jefferson himself expressed the opinion that no one, except the leader of our Revolutionary army, could establish and maintain the new government against those opposed to it. (*Letter to Mr. Hopkinson, March,* 1789.) Above all, it should be remembered that Washington had labored more efficiently than any other person, to achieve that very liberty which his assailants persistently charged him with seeking to subvert. Jefferson did not venture openly or directly to asperse the man, whom a grateful people designated and recognized as "the father of his country." The attacks were made in private letters, and through the agency of others; the most malignant calumniators were foreign adventurers. For years before the batteries of detraction were opened, and during the whole time their fire was continued, Jefferson professed friendship and admiration for Washington, sometimes in terms indicative of veneration. Here are the proofs.

On May 28th, 1781, Jefferson, then Governor of Virginia, wrote to the General-in-Chief of the army, asking him to come in person and expel the British troops from the State. In this letter, the Governor thus appeals to the General: "Your appearance among them (Virginians) would restore full confidence of salvation, and render them equal to whatever is not impossible." He adds that the General's presence would give the writer "an additional motive (*which I thought could not have been*) for that gratitude, esteem, and respect which I have long felt for your excellency." In March, 1789, he wrote Mr. F. Hopkinson that Washington's "executive talents are superior, I believe, to those of any man in the world," and alluded to "his perfect integrity." On March 27th, 1791, he thus addresses Washington himself: "For your safety, no one on earth more sincerely prays than I, both for public and private regards." The letter containing his resignation of the Secretaryship of State, dated December 31st, 1793, closes as follows: "I carry into my retirement a lively sense of your goodness, and shall continue gratefully to remember it. With my serious prayers for your life, health, and tranquillity, I pray you to accept the homage of the great and constant respect and attachment with which I have the honor to be, etc." Compare these humbly affectionate words with the bitter and contemptuous language respecting the President, found in the letter to Madison, written just one year afterwards, in regard to the Democratic societies and the repression of the Whiskey Revolt.

On June 10th, 1796, the *Aurora* published the questions concerning our relations with France, that were confidentially submitted to the Cabinet when Jefferson was Secretary of State, and of which, as Washington knew, the ex-Secretary had a copy. On June 19th, Jefferson, then at Monticello, addressed to Washington a letter, in which he disavowed with vehement asseverations of sincerity, any connection with the publication. In that letter, he takes occasion to express his undiminished regard for the President, and continues: "I learn that this last (General H. Lee) has thought it worth while to try to sow tares between you and me, by representing me as still engaged in turbulence and intrigue against the government. I never believed for a moment that this could make any impression on you, or that your knowledge of me would not outweigh the slander of an intriguer." It will be remembered that he expressed similar sentiments, and employed some of these very phrases in a letter to Aaron Burr, written in 1801, a few days before the balloting for President began in the House of Representatives. After very affectionate compliments to Mrs. Washington, he concludes in these terms: "I have the honor to be, with great and sincere esteem and respect, dear sir, your most obedient and most humble servant." Two months before, he had written the Mazzei letter.

We learn from Jefferson himself that his last meeting with Washington was at the inauguration of Mr. Adams; that his parting on that occasion "was warmly affectionate, and I never had reason to believe any change on his part, as there certainly was none on mine." (*Letter to Mr. Van Buren, June 29th*, 1824.) In May, 1797, the Mazzei letter appeared in this country. Jefferson privately admitted that the letter as published was substantially what he had written to Mazzei, except "in one place," but upon consultation with his friends, decided not to avow or disavow his authorship of it.

Some twenty-seven years after, Timothy Pickering stated, in his *Review of the Correspondence between John Adams and William Cunningham,* that Washington demanded in writing from Jefferson a disavowal of this letter, or an apology for it. It was for the purpose of denying this statement, and showing its improbability, that the letter to Van Buren was written. In that letter, Jefferson declares that no apology was made or demanded; that no correspondence in regard to the Mazzei letter was exchanged between himself and Washington; that the expression, "Samsons in the field," found therein, referred to the Cincinnati generally, and that Washington had no cause to be offended, and was not offended at the contents of the letter. But in writing to Madison, August 3d, 1797, he assigns as one of the chief reasons for not avowing the letter, the apprehension that such avowal would "bring on a personal difference between General Washington and myself. It would embroil me, too, with all those with whom his character is still popular, that is, with nine-tenths of the people of the United States." The letters mentioned by Mr. Pickering were not found among Washington's papers, after his death. They, who allege the correspondence, say the letters were probably abstracted by some one, possibly by Tobias Lear, Washington's private secretary. Jefferson maintained a confidential intercourse with Lear, and soon after his accession to the Presidency, gave him a diplomatic appointment.

Early in the year 1798, John Nicholas, of Virginia, informed Washington by mail that there was in the Charlottesville Post Office a letter addressed in his hand-writing to John Langhorne. Mr. Nicholas further stated that no person of that name resided in that vicinity, or, to the best of his knowledge, in the County, and that he feared some one had laid a snare for the ex-President. Washington answered that, a short time before, he had received a letter, dated Warren, Albemarle county, Va., and signed John Langhorne, in which the writer condoled with him in the aspersions to which he was subjected, and hoped he would not permit them to disturb his peace of mind, and that he had replied to it. He sent Mr. Nicholas a copy of the letter and of the reply. Mr. Nicholas learned that the Langhorne letter was taken from the post office by a political opponent of Washington, it would seem by a messenger from Monticello.

After further investigations, Mr. Nicholas wrote another letter to Washington. This letter has not been published, but some idea of its contents may be formed from Washington's answer, dated March 8th, 1798. In this he writes: "Nothing short of the evidence you have adduced, corroborative of intimations which I had received long before through another channel, could have shaken my belief in the sincerity of a friendship, which I conceived was possessed for me by the person (Jefferson) to whom you allude." His belief in a friendship, attested by the repeated and deferential declarations of a person so trusted, and bound to him by so many ties as was Mr. Jefferson, must, indeed, have been hard to shake. The fact that John Nicholas was a zealous and somewhat prominent member of the political party opposed to him, had probably much weight with Washington. It is proper to state that Jefferson, when he wrote Mr. Van Buren the letter in which he endeavored to show that he retained Washington's confidence to the end, was ignorant of the correspondence between the latter and Mr. Nicholas.

CHAPTER XIX.

JEFFERSON'S OPINION OF RIOTS AND INSURRECTIONS.

From Paris, on December 20th, 1787, he wrote to Mr. Madison "The late rebellion in Massachusetts (Shay's) has given more alarm than it should have done. Calculate that one rebellion in thirteen States, in the course of eleven years, is but one for each State, in a century and a half. No country should be so long without one."

In a letter to Mr. Madison of December 28th, 1794, he refers to the Whiskey Insurrection of Western Pennsylvania. Far from blaming the insurgents, he excuses them; calls them "our friends;" styles the Excise law that caused the revolt, "an infernal one;" condemns, in very strong terms, the violent means employed for its suppression; censures the Government for its decisive action in the matter; ridicules the troops it sent; says the detestation of the law is universal, and has extended itself to the Government; and finally declares that "*separation is now near and certain, and determined in the mind of every man.*" In a word, his indignation is stirred, not by the insurrection, but by its suppression. The insurgents attacked with a force of 500 men the house of the inspector of the revenue, and a detachment of United States troops sent for its defence; burned the house, and forced the officer in command of the troops to march out and surrender; shot at the U. S. Marshal while in the performance of his duty; seized him and endeavored to intimidate him; violated the United States mail; banished from Pittsburgh citizens whom they suspected of allegiance to the government; declared their purpose to resist by violence every attempt to enforce the obnoxious law, and, to carry out this purpose, raised a force of seven thousand men; rejected an amnesty proffered by the President, and set on foot measures for the dissolution of the Union, in case other methods of nullifying the law should prove abortive. The conspiracy extended over Western Pennsylvania, Western Maryland, and parts of Virginia. Some of its agencies were established in the very suburbs of Philadelphia. One of the leaders said that if much pressed, they might march on the seat of the National Government. So great was the prevalent sense of danger in the disturbed districts, that even Quakers volunteered to fight against the insurgents. Such was the rebellion that Jefferson palliated, styling it merely "riotous transactions," and excusing it, on the ground that the Excise law was objectionable. His own State shamed him by a ready response to the President's call for volunteers, and her Governor, General Lee, accepted the position of commander-in-chief of the troops called out for the suppression of the insurrection.

Jefferson wrote from Paris to Edward Carrington, January 16th, 1787, "To punish these *errors* (tumults in the Eastern States) too severely would be to *suppress the only safeguard of the public liberty.*" On January 30th, 1787, he writes to Mr. Carrington, "A little rebellion now and then is as necessary in the political world, as storms in the physical;" "Governors should be so mild in their punishment of rebellions as not to discourage them too much. It is a medicine, necessary for the sound health of the government."

Writing to Colonel Smith, he exclaims: "*God forbid we should ever be twenty years without such a rebellion!* (as

Shay's) .... What country can preserve its liberties, if its rulers are not warned from time to time that this people preserve the spirit of resistance? Let them take arms. The remedy is to set them right as to facts, pardon and pacify them. .... *The tree of liberty must be refreshed from time to time with the blood of patriots and tyrants.* It is its natural manure."

CHAPTER XX.

SOME EVIDENCE OF HIS INSINCERITY.

A CLOSE observer of men has remarked, "Beware of him, who places his hand over his heart, when he makes a statement or a promise." The same caution should be exercised in regard to him who habitually employs asseveration in writing or speaking. Jefferson frequently did this. He protested "In the name of Heaven," that he made no effort to control the sentiments or the conduct of the *National Gazette.* In the Virginia Convention of 1775, he declared "By the God that made me, I will cease to exist, before I yield to such a connection with England, and on such terms as the British Parliament propose." When he was about to relate an incident derogatory to Hamilton, in the introduction to his *Ana,* he prefaced the relation by the words: "For the truth of which (this) I attest the God who made me." When he expressed, in a letter to Adams, the pleasure which the latter's election to the Presidency afforded him, he appealed to his neighbors for confirmation of what he wrote.

Truth, in her narrations, resorts to no oaths, expletives, or attestations; her language is simple, her communications are yea, yea, and nay, nay. The asseverations of Jefferson weaken rather than strengthen his declarations. They awaken doubts of his sincerity. Accordingly, one is not surprised to find in his life and writings, exhibitions of the opposite quality. Some of them we mention.

1. He received Lafayette cordially, with protestations of

gratitude and friendship. Very soon thereafter, he wrote that the Frenchman had a "Canine thirst for popularity ;" —this in a letter to Madison.

2. He styled kings "human lions, tigers, and mammoths," not once, but several times during his writings. On April 6th, 1790, he pronounced Louis XVI. "A prince, the model of Royal excellence," and otherwise eulogized him. He also praised Alexander I., of Russia, almost fulsomely, in a letter addressed to him in 1805.

3. He more than once expressed a wish to "*extirpate from creation*," the royal lions, tigers, and mammoths aforesaid, whom he sometimes transformed into "vermin." Yet the letter to the Czar, above mentioned, thus closes: "By monuments of such offices, may your life become an epoch in the history of the condition of men, and may He who called it into being for the good of the human family, *give it length of days and success, and have it always in his holy keeping.*" This letter was not called forth by the demands of hospitality, diplomacy, or gratitude for some great national assistance, such as that rendered us by France, but was Jefferson's spontaneous tribute to one of the "imperial vermin."

4. When he quitted the gubernatorial chair of Virginia, he solemnly expressed his fixed resolution never to return to public life. *The very next year*, he accepted an office under the general government, and was afterwards, successively Minister at the court of Versailles, Secretary of State, Vice-President, and President for two terms.

5. On May 14th, 1794, he wrote Washington, "I cherish tranquillity too much to suffer political things to enter my mind at all." In the following December, he penned that letter to Madison, in which he rails at the President for his expressed disapprobation of the Democratic societies.

This letter reveals Jefferson's familiarity with public affairs, and his profound interest in the "things" to which he professed entire indifference, as well as the undiminished intensity of his political feelings, for he therein designates the Senate as the " Augean herd."

6. In the letter last mentioned, dated December 28th, 1794, are found these words, " I would not give up my retirement *for the empire of the universe.*" In less than twelve months, Jefferson was recognized by the leaders of his party as the Republican candidate for the Presidency, and was voted for as such by his party friends at the election in October, 1796. The electoral votes cast for him, did not elevate him to the Presidency, but were numerous enough to make him Vice-President. This office he did not decline, and he soon left his retirement for an authority not quite so extensive as the empire of the universe.

7. Only four months prior to this election, he pretended in a letter to Washington that he was taking no part in political affairs, in fact that he had an aversion to them. " Political conversations " wrote this ambitious man, " I actually dislike, and avoid, when I can without affectation."

8. When this result of the election was ascertained, he wrote Mr. Adams the President-elect, that he "never wished any other issue" of the contest. He had consented to be put forward as a candidate for the Presidency, his party friends had voted for him, and endeavored to elect him; he had watched their efforts in his behalf, he knew how earnestly they desired his success, but he never wished to be chosen, and was pleased at his and their failure. He was a zealous Republican, opposed to any increase of Federal power, and fearful that we were tending towards the English form of government. Adams was a leading Federalist, in favor of a strong central government, and one of

those most seriously afflicted with that "Anglomania" which so much alarmed Jefferson; yet he was gratified by Adams's election, and never wished any other result.

That Adams would doubt this astonishing statement Jefferson knew, and referred therefore to his neighbors for attestation of his sincerity. He wrote: "And though I shall not be believed, yet it is not the less true, that I never wished any other (issue). My neighbors, as my compurgators, could aver this fact as seeing my occupations and my attachment to them." Does a man conscious of his own sincerity, anticipate that his statement will be disbelieved, and bring forward his "compurgators," before his truthfulness is questioned? Not only was he glad that Adams was chosen, but he intimated that he would not be displeased at the re-election of his late opponent. Surely, more compurgation is needed here.

This letter is so fine a specimen of Jefferson's epistolary excellence, that it merits special attention. Though he states therein that "in the retired canton" wherein he lives, "we know little of what is passing," he is aware that "The public, and the public papers have been much occupied lately in placing us in a point of opposition to each other." He then says the issue of the contest was not known at Philadelphia on the 16th of December, the date of his latest advices from that city, thus leaving the impression that he was still ignorant of the result, but it is manifest from the whole letter, that he was positively informed of it. He proceeds to declare that he never wished any other issue. Then follows this skilful, Machiavelian combination of words. "It is possible, indeed, that even you may be cheated out of your succession by a trick worthy of the subtlety of your arch friend of New York, who has been able to make of your real friends tools for defeating their and your just wishes. Probably, however, he will be disappointed as to you; and my inclinations put me out of his reach." In this passage, Jefferson would induce Adams to believe that he and his friends have a right to expect his re-election, that he will be chosen for a second term, unless Aaron Burr cheats him out of the succession, that the writer will not be his competitor, and will be gratified by his re-election. By thus addressing him, Jefferson would probably achieve the following results; he would learn whether Adams desired a re-election, and his opinion in regard to the probability of such re-election; he would ascertain whether Adams regarded Burr favorably, or unfavorably, and also whether the former expected the latter to be a candidate at the ensuing presidential election; he would secure the sympathy if not the support of Adams, in case he did not desire a second term, and Jefferson's friends should bring him forward: should Adams seek a re-election, and Jefferson also aspire to the Presidential chair, he could more effectually mature his plans, and carry on his campaign, when the attention of his adversary was diverted from his movements. Finally, he would earn the favor, perhaps the gratitude of Adams, for use in future emergencies.

His letter next expresses his preference for private over public life. "I have no ambition," says he philosophically, "to govern men. It is a painful and thankless office. .... I leave to others the sublime delights of exalted station." He declares that his election to the Presidency in the recent contest, would have been "oppressive" to him. He sets forth his love of retirement, and his aversion to high position so strongly, that a person who should read the letter without any knowledge of the writer, might well believe that he would have refused to serve, had he been chosen President, and wonder why he did not resign the

Vice-Presidency. He proceeds to say that his "sincere prayer" is that Mr. Adams's administration " may be filled with glory and happiness" to himself, and advantage to the country. He concludes by assuring the President-elect that the writer retains for him "solid esteem," and "sentiments of sincere respect and attachment." This letter can be fully appreciated only by a careful perusal of the whole of it, while bearing in mind, the party and personal alienation of Jefferson from Adams, prior to the election. It has been supposed, that it was written in order that Jefferson might be invited to share the deliberations of the cabinet, which he much desired to do. This was possibly its immediate object, but its ulterior aim was undoubtedly much higher.

Jefferson's repugnance to official life, and ardent love of retirement did not prevent him from entering upon the duties of the Vice-Presidency at the appointed time, March 4th, 1797. Before doing so, he had consulted with Mr. Madison, as to the proper method of using the new President for the interest of the Republican party. He soon began to intrigue for the "succession." As usual he worked in secret, by means of private letters. His first tentative missive of which we have a copy, was written to Adam's "arch friend" Burr, in regard to national affairs, with an incidental allusion to the state of the party, and its prospects in New York. This letter, dated June 17th, expresses gloomy apprehensions for the safety of free institutions among us, and intimates that unless the Federalists be expelled from power, the Revolutionary war would have been fought in vain. He asks Burr's opinion on these subjects.

On June 24th, he despatched a letter to Governor Rutledge of South Carolina, wherein he pours forth lamentations over the condition of affairs, and sighs for the repose of private life. He writes, "This is, indeed, a most humiliating state of things, but it commenced in 1793." .... "We had in 1793 the most respectable character in the universe. But matters have been growing worse and worse, and now, we are low, indeed, with the belligerents. Their kicks and cuffs prove their contempt;" which, being interpreted, means "this humiliation has been brought upon us by the party in power. Don't you think, my friend, there ought to be a change?" He deplores the violence of political passions. "Tranquility," he continues, "is the old man's milk. I go to enjoy it, in a few days, and to exchange the roar of bulls and bears for the prattle of my grandchildren and senile rest."

As we read these words we pity the gentle old man, burdened with the cares of office, and weary of the strife of contending factions. But pity pauses, when it is suggested to her that these words, addressed to the Governor, are intended for his political brother, General Pinckney, who may possibly be one of the Federalist candidates at the next Presidential election. She is transformed into another sentiment, when she perceives that Jefferson's "senile rest" means more than his wonted activity in political manœuvres, and that his letters to confidential friends evince a spirit quite different from that of his communication to Rutledge. In it there is an almost "ethereal mildness." To Mr. Madison, he denounced the President's first message as "inflammatory," and characterized the message, recommending that the country be put in a state of defence, as "insane." He calls the friends of the President "War Hawks," "Adamites," "Anglo-men;" declares that his alleged reasons for martial preparations are not plausible enough "to impose upon the weakest mind," and arraigns the administration for "violations of the Constitution, propensities to war, to expense and to a particular foreign connection." He contemptuously says that Mr. Adams' answers to the addresses that pour in upon him are "more thrasonical than the addresses themselves," and informs Madison that the advocates of a war with France "talk of *Septembrizing*, deportation, and the examples of quelling sedition set by the French Executive."* Instead of resting contented with the prattle of his grandchildren, he wrote a long confession of his political faith to Mr. Gerry; denounced the Alien and Sedition laws; inveighed against the "usurpations" of the Federal Judiciary, and proposed measures for checking them; opposed the punishment of journalistic libellers; discussed the question of the impeachment of Senators; watched with keen interest the negotiations with France, and with a still keener interest the home political field; prepared the very elaborate "resolutions of '98," and procured their adoption (in modified form) by the Legislatures of Kentucky and Virginia; had portions of them a second time proposed to those Legislatures; urged Madison, Monroe, Gerry, and the aged Pendleton, of Virginia, to attack Federalism or vindicate Republicanism through the press, but published not a line of his own production. In a word, he directed the operations of his party throughout the Union, and that so efficient, as to place it in control of the government.

Is it possible that he, who said and did these things, is the same person who penned the letter of December 28th, 1796, to Mr. Adams? It is even so. In that letter, Jefferson stated that his "sincere prayer" was that the administration of the President-elect might "be filled with glory and happiness to him." Yet he used every means to assail and weaken that administration, and bring it into hatred and contempt. In that letter, he intimated to Adams that

---

* The reader will bear in mind that Jefferson was Vice-President, when he thus disparaged the President and his friends.

he would not be displeased at his re-election. Yet he strained every nerve to prevent that re-election. In that letter, he more than intimated that he would not be Adams' competitor in the contest for the Presidency, yet he was such competitor. In it, he expressed strong aversion to high office, especially to that of President, and affirmed that he left "to others the sublime delights" of that exalted position, yet he so managed affairs that his own nomination was inevitable. He did not decline when nominated, but manifested an earnest desire for election, notably, when the choice devolved upon the House of Representatives; he was elected, and served his term with no hint of resignation. The retention of the letter by Mr. Madison, to whom it was intrusted with discretion to retain or deliver it, does not all affect one's opinion of its author.

9. On June 19th, 1796, Jefferson wrote Washington: " I learn that this last (General H. Lee) has thought it worth while to try to sow tares between you and me, by representing me as still engaged in the bustle of politics, and in turbulence and intrigue against the government." He adds that he did not think it his duty, in case public questions were introduced at table, to abstain from expressing his opinions merely because he had been a member of the Cabinet. Then, to show how completely he was weaned from politics, he discusses " pease and clover " and the " Carolina drill." In this letter, Jefferson indignantly disclaims all attention to political affairs, or concern in them, and appeals to Washington's knowledge of his character in confirmation of his statements; yet on the preceding April 24th, he had written the Mazzei letter, filled with abuse and denunciation of his political opponents. On June 12th, seven days before the letter to Washington, he wrote to Mr. Monroe that "Congress have risen. . . . One man (the

President) outweighs them all in influence over the people. ... Republicanism must lie on its oars. We are completely saddled and bridled" by the Federalists. He points out that there must soon be a change, and exhorts Monroe in the meantime to be patient. On July 10th, he again writes Monroe respecting the political situation. These three letters certainly do not evince an entire unconcern about political matters. When one reads them, and remembers that in October of the same year Jefferson was elected Vice-President, it is hard to believe, notwithstanding his disclaimer, that he was not "still engaged in the bustle of politics."

10. Although he had slandered Hamilton, he told Mr. Thomas M. Bayley that he was really the friend of Hamilton.

11. In his letters to Aaron Burr, Jefferson professed esteem, regard, and friendship for him. In his secret archives, he recorded that Burr was venal, and unworthy of confidence.

12. He publicly expressed indignation mingled with horror against those, who wrote or spoke favorably of the English Government. Privately, he wrote to John Adams that the "English Constitution is acknowledged to be better than all which have preceded it."

13. In his *Ana* is this entry: "I have never done a single act, or been concerned in any transaction, which I feared to have fully laid open." This was part of an alleged conversation with Burr. His correspondence by no means substantiates this declaration. Many of his letters contain an injunction of secrecy, others, intimations that they are confidential. So anxious was he to conceal some of his transactions, that he did not venture to intrust communications respecting them to the mails, but retained them

until they could be transmitted by reliable private messengers.

14. In writing to Washington himself, or to his known friends, as well as in personal intercourse with him, Jefferson evinced a profound admiration for the General, and seemed greatly pleased by his esteem and approbation. But he secretly intrigued against him, disparaged him in letters to his enemies, and, it would seem, scandalously defamed him through the agency of others. For fifteen years, Jefferson hoodwinked this renowned man, his friend and benefactor, who was too frank himself to suspect insincerity in others.

15. He censured Adams and Hamilton for aspiring to high official position, upon the ground that such aspiration was a departure from those principles of equality without which liberty could not exist—that a man had no right to desire authority over other men. At the same time, he was secretly working and planning for his own elevation to power.

16. But perhaps the strongest evidence of Jefferson's insincerity is to be found in the contrast between his public, and his private expressions of opinion concerning the people. During the greatest part of his life, he publicly asserted their incorruptible virtue; he maintained the wisdom of their judgment, and treated their wishes with the utmost deference; he was ever on the alert to detect and thwart some real or imaginary infraction of their liberties; he loudly proclaimed the dignity and grandeur of human nature. In his own time, he was greeted by the multitude as "the people's friend;" he is, to-day, regarded as the apostle and champion of popular rights, and venerated as the "Father of American Democracy." Yet his letters to his intimate friends abound in sentiments concerning the multitude, quite opposite to those publicly expressed, and

show that he really entertained a profound contempt for mankind.

These letters contain repeated declarations of the deceptions practiced by priests upon the people in all ages and countries. The assertion of these deceptions is a denial of the intelligence of the people. In 1785, he writes, "*I consider the class of artificers as the panders of vice;* the instruments by which the liberties of a country are generally overturned." He complained of the ingratitude of the people, when they blamed his incompetency at the time of the invasion of Virginia, while he was Governor. Further evidence of his low estimate of his fellow-men is found in his oft expressed disbelief in the sincerity of those, whose political or religious opinions differed from his own; in his imputing improper motives to his political opponents, and in his allegations that they stooped to base means to promote the success of their principles.

In his letter of March 29th, 1801, to Mr. Gerry, he attributes mercenary motives to all ministers of religion, and to the editors of the Federal journals. He therein charges his leading political opponents in New England with prostituting government, religion, and justice to the promotion of their schemes, and with deluding the people. While asserting that the delusion has been greater there than elsewhere, he admits a popular political delusion throughout the country. This letter alone would suffice to show the insincerity of Jefferson's professions of regard for the people, and his distrust of their ability for self-government, since it reveals his opinion that most of their political, and all their religious, leaders are mercenary, selfish impostors, and that the rest of the community is liable to be duped by these impostors. Yet in this very letter, he flatters the people, tells Mr. Gerry that "they will wake like Samson from his sleep, and carry away the gates and posts of the city," and that "you, my friend, are destined to rally them." If they had been deluded by the Federalists, why should not the Republicans practice upon them, especially as they were in the latter case, to be deceived for their own welfare? On January 16th, 1787, he writes to Edward Carrington, "Man is the only animal that devours his own kind." In a letter to Jedediah Morse, he alludes to the enormities of the French Jacobins and thus continues: "Yet these were men, and we and our descendants will be no more. The present is a case *where we are to guard against ourselves*, not against ourselves as we are, but as we may be, for who can now imagine what we may become under circumstances not now imaginable?" In 1821, he wrote to John Adams "what a bedlamite is man?"

In a letter to Mann Page, dated August 30th, 1795, he paints the upper classes as dishonest, the lower as contemptible. He says: "I have always found the rogues would be uppermost, and I do not know that the proportion mentioned by Montaigne, fourteen-fifteenths, is too strong for the higher orders, and for those who rising above the *swinish multitude*, always contrive to nestle themselves in the places of power." Mr. Jefferson's preference that the Representatives in Congress should be chosen by the Legislatures, rather than by the people, has been mentioned under another head. Writing to an intimate friend, respecting a work called *The Political Progress*, he thus expresses himself: "They (this and another work) disgust me indeed by opening to my view *the ulcerated state of the human mind*. The reflections into which it leads us are not very flattering to the human species. In the whole animal kingdom, I recollect no family but man, steadily and systematically employed in the destruction of itself. Nor does what is called civilization produce any other effect, than to teach him to pursue the principle of the *bellum omnium inter omnia*, on a greater scale, and instead of the little contests between tribe and tribe, to comprehend all the quarters of the earth in the same work of destruction. If to this we add, that as to other animals, the lions and tigers are mere lambs compared with man as a destroyer, we must conclude that nature has been able to find in man alone, a sufficient barrier against the too great multiplication of other animals, and of man himself."

No enemy of popular rights, no haughty tyrant, no professed misanthropist, would probably place a lower estimate on his fellow-creatures than does this vaunted friend of the people, in his private letters. He believes that men are imbeciles, liable to be duped by every impostor; that they are bedlamites, perpetually engaged in the work of destroying each other; that the upper classes are rogues; the lower, "a swinish multitude;" that their state is so "ulcerated" as to excite disgust. Worst of all, he sees no prospect of their emerging from their present degradation. In his opinion, *civilization only enables these miserable beings to maim and murder on a larger scale,* and "we and our descendants" are liable to become even such as the Jacobin butchers of the French Revolution. Had Jefferson never written a letter, the hollowness of his professions of attachment to the people might have been inferred. His aristocratic birth and associations, his refined tastes, his studious habits, his love of tranquility, his peculiar sensitiveness, all combined to preclude the possibility of his hearty sympathy with the rude and ignorant populace.

CHAPTER XXI.

JEFFERSON AND THE FRENCH REVOLUTION.

In a letter, dated January 3d, 1793, and addressed to James Short, he thus writes of that Revolution. "In the struggle, which was necessary, many guilty persons fell without the forms of law, and with them, some innocent. These I deplore as much as anybody, but I deplore them as I should have done had they fallen in battle. It was necessary to use the arm of the people, a machine, not quite so blind as balls and bombs, *but blind to a certain degree.* A few of their innocent friends met at their hands the fate of enemies, but time and truth will rescue and embalm their memories, while their posterity will be enjoying that liberty for which they would never have hesitated to offer up their lives. The liberty of the whole earth was depending on the issue of the contest, and was ever such a prize won with so little innocent blood?" He then states that his affections were wounded by the loss of some who perished in the Revolution, and continues: "Rather than it should have failed, I would have seen *half of the earth desolated. Were there but an Adam and Eve left in every country,* if left free, it would be better than it now is." Not only did Jefferson entertain these senseless and atrocious sentiments, but in the same letter he *declared that they were held by ninety-nine hundredths of the people* in the United States. So anxious was he to conceal from his fellow-citizens the contents of the letter, in which this shocking allegation is made, that he more than once mentioned to Mr. Short its private nature, and caused it to be sent through the Spanish legation.

During the Reign of Terror in France, the painter, David, wished to have the number of daily executions increased. It is related, that in communicating this wish to the Revolutionary Tribunal, he employed metaphorically an expression familiar to the votaries of his own beautiful art, and said with fiendish humor: "We must *grind in a little more red.*" Collot d'Herbois, during the orgie of blood at Lyons, slew, in one day, fifteen hundred of his fellow-creatures. Marat, the tawny tyrant, whom Charlotte Corday smote to death, recommended the slaughter of 270,000 human victims, in order to insure the triumph of liberty. Another friend of liberty, equality, and fraternity, proposed to mount the guillotine on wheels, so as to expedite the work of death. We shudder at these inhuman deeds, and execrate the savages who performed or proposed them. What then shall be thought of Jefferson, who rather than the French Revolution should have failed, would have seen half the earth made desolate, nay, would have been content to have but two persons left in each country?

CHAPTER XXII.

EFFECTS OF HIS LIFE AND DOCTRINES.

"The evil that men do lives after them." Many of the ills that now afflict the body politic, have sprung from the life and writings of Jefferson. One of his theories, brooded over by the spirit of that State Sovereignty fanatic, John C. Calhoun, brought forth the two abortions, nullification, and secession, and drenched the land in fraternal blood. Another, preached and applied by unscrupulous men, greedy for popularity, has unfurled the flag of repudiation in eight states of the Union; has fixed the stigma of financial dishonor upon the venerable "Mother of presidents;" has so perverted and blinded another great State, that, though rich and abundantly able to discharge all her obligations, she sent forth agents to compound with her creditors, and squander in useless expeditions funds that should have been expended in payment of her debts. These agents quartered themselves at the best hotels, "fared sumptuously every day," and, bewitched by the hag that had corrupted their State, into the delusion that they were engaged in a laudable business, with heads erect and self-satisfied air, announced that the proud Commonwealth, which they represented, had magnanimously consented to return to her helpless creditors a little more than one-half of the money, that they loaned her on the security of her honor.

Jefferson's political philosophy awakened a desire for power in the meanest individuals. He and his partisans taught that there was not only "a universal right, but a universal capacity to govern. Advantages of education and morals were denied, and to fill an inferior place in society was the result not of an inferior ability, but of less courage and weaker purpose." The drunken and ribald Paine was adduced to show that infidelity and insubordination opened a short road to distinction. To Jefferson mainly we owe it, that public stations of trust and responsibility are often occupied by the incompetent and the unworthy; that the sacred interests of education are frequently confided to ignorant and unprincipled men; that demagogues ride triumphantly to places of distinction, and that political corruption prevails in the land. "To him mainly we owe it, that the hireling of party finds reason for the denial of justice in the opinions of the applicant;" that so little respect is entertained for our legal tribunals; that a pure and venerable Chief Justice of the Supreme Court was ridiculed, taunted, and denounced for his opinion in the Dred Scott case; that three Justices of the same Court have been repeatedly charged with disregarding law while members of the Electoral Commission, and deciding according to their political predilections; that any contemptible scribbler is at liberty, unrebuked, to criticise and declare void the decisions of the most learned and august tribunal, and that he is often applauded for the exercise of that liberty.

Are these things so? Has the judicial ermine been dragged in the mire of partisan politics? Has the title of Judge, formerly so revered, been almost shorn of honor? Has one Judge been shot in Kentucky, by a litigant whom his interpretation of the law displeased? Has one been killed in Texas for a similar reason, and have other ministers of justice in that State been threatened with a like fate, unless certain anticipated decisions are satisfactory? All this, though shameful, is scarcely surprising, for the man whom the people delight to honor, from whose lips they gladly receive instruction, and who is the political oracle of many, denounced some of the rulings of Chief Justice Marshall, and asserted that they encouraged treason and protected traitors; pardoned one or more convicts, not because he believed they had not committed the offences charged, but because he deemed unconstitutional the law under which they were convicted; declared that he would not be guided in his official actions by the decisions of the Supreme Court, and most offensively styled the Federal judiciary, "A corps of sappers and miners, working underground, to undermine the foundations of our confederate fabric."

Is sedition fostered to the overthrow of the law? Is armed resistance to constituted authority regarded as a legitimate method of securing the redress of real or imaginary grievances? Are "strikes," attended with intimidation and violence, winked at and encouraged? Is a riot a frequent means of obtaining an increase of wages? Is a powerful combination, obstructing by force and arms the great avenues of trade and travel, and creating a panic in every department of business, but a trivial affair? Is a mob, usurping the functions of the legally appointed officers, and ruthlessly hanging in hot blood the innocent and the guilty, too often with shocking cruelty, mildly condemned, or half approved, instead of being universally denounced? Did one of these blind agents of popular vengeance, at the very doors of a Court-House, tear from the custody of the sheriff ten men and murder them? Have these incidents of a half-civilized society, gradually extended themselves from our new Western communities, where the machinery of government is yet but imperfect, to the older States where all the appliances for the lawful punishment of crime are found in full operation? Are the participants in these unlawful and demoralizing outbreaks seldom punished? For this lamentable state of affairs, the responsibility, in great part, rests upon him who taught that rioters should be lightly dealt with; that they should generally be pardoned and pacified.

In a word, the life, the doctrines, and the extraordinary influence of Thomas Jefferson have done more than the life, doctrines and influence of any other individual, living or dead, to produce and foster the restlessness, the self-assertion, the restiveness under parental control, the diminished reverence for all that is sacred and venerable, the contempt of lawful authority, human and Divine, the spirit of insubordination, the tendency to turbulence, that now exist among us, filling thoughtful minds with gloomy apprehensions in regard to the future of our country. Verily, "The evil that men do lives after them."

www.ingramcontent.com/pod-product-compliance
Lightning Source LLC
Chambersburg PA
CBHW020254170426
43202CB00008B/365